DEDICATION.

TO

THE EMPRESS CARLOTTA,

THE recollection of whose unwearied labors and affectionate solicitude for their prosperity and happiness, will be forever cherished in the hearts of the Mexican people,

This volume is

Respectfully dedicated by

THE AUTHOR.

MEXICO

UNDER

MAXIMILIAN.

BY
HENRY M. FLINT, Esq.,
AUTHOR OF "DRUID'S LETTERS," "LIFE OF SENATOR DOUGLAS," ETC.

NATIONAL PUBLISHING COMPANY,
PHILADELPHIA, PA.; BOSTON, MASS.; RICHMOND, VA.; CINCINNATI, OHIO; CHICAGO, ILL.; ST. LOUIS, MO.; ATLANTA, GA.; NEW ORLEANS, LA.

PREFACE.

THE object of the author, in writing this book, is to remove if possible, to some extent, the prejudice which exists against the present government of Mexico. This prejudice is based upon a misapprehension of the character of that government; and upon the fact that very little is known, in the United States, of what Maximilian has done for Mexico. If any intelligent citizen of the United States should go to that country, remain there for six months, make himself somewhat acquainted with the Mexican people, and see with his own eyes how much Maximilian has done for their happiness and prosperity, and, above all, compare Mexico under a monarchy with what it always has been under a republic, he would candidly admit that at last Mexico has found the government that is suited to her, and that will eventually raise her to a respectable rank among the nations of the earth. The government of Maximilian is a limited constitutional monarchy; it is founded upon the choice of the Mexican people; and, in spite of the difficulties which it has had to contend with, and which environ it now, it has done more for the prosperity of Mexico; more for the enlightenment and happiness of the Mexican people, during the three years of its existence, than any republican government in Mexico ever did, in thirty, forty, or fifty, years.

It is possible that this book may be unpopular. I do not write for popularity, however, but to set forth the truth. From the foundation of the republic up to the year 1861, independence of thought was considered creditable, and freedom of speech and of the press were regarded as the most precious birth-rights of an American citizen. From the foundation of the republic up to the year 1861, the man who had not manliness of soul enough to think for himself, and courage enough to express his thoughts frankly, was despised. No character was more contemptible than one who slavishly copied the opinions of others, and had no opinions of his own.

This is all changed now. We live under a new and "loyal" dispensation. In 1861 and 1862, the edict went forth that men must stop thinking for themselves, and must stop expressing their thoughts. All men must think alike; and they must think in a "loyal" manner. To believe that the war against the south was unnecessary, and might have been avoided; to believe that it would end in the destruction of the Union, and to express that belief, was "disloyal." To believe that the withholding of medicines from the sick in the south was cruel, and to express that belief, was "disloyal." To believe that the object of the war on the part of the north, was the subjugation and conquest of the Southern States and the permanent dissolution of the Union, and to express that belief, was "treason." To believe that Abraham Lincoln was neither a saint nor a statesman, and to express that belief, was to be a "traitor." In a word, every one was required to believe as the leaders of the radical Republican party believed, and to speak as they spoke. Whoever did not do so, was a marked man.

It was thus that the ideas about the Mexican empire sprang up. Napoleon is helping the south. Napoleon is going to recognize the Southern Confederacy. Napoleon has established a monarchy in Mexico, to which he will annex Texas, and to this will be annexed, in time, all the Southern States. This was the first song; and nobody was allowed to sing in a different tune. Then, again, Napoleon is helping the south. Napoleon is going to recognize the south. The throne of Maximilian is upheld by the presence of French troops, and a French army is to be permanently maintained in Mexico. This was the next song. Everybody's violin, flute, harp, sackbut, and dulcimer, must play the same notes, and smashed be the fiddle that will not. Then, again, well, at any rate, Napoleon desired to help the south, and wished to recognize the Southern Confederacy. The establishment of a monarchy in Mexico was a part of the rebellion. We crushed the one; now we must crush the other. This is the present radical song, which they have been singing ever since the close of the war. It is founded upon the same wise principles of statesmanship as the bill of Mr. Thaddeus Stevens for changing the ten Southern States into five Military Departments.

That this book has many imperfections, I am well aware. The materials, accessible for the work, have not been abundant; nor have I enjoyed the opportunity of devoting to it that continuous and uninterrupted labor without which no literary work can be free from faults. I commend it, however, to an indulgent public, with the sincere hope that it may dispel many of the delusions that have prevailed in relation to the Mexican empire.

H. M. F.

WASHINGTON, FEB. 22, 1867.

CONTENTS.

CHAPTER I.

CHAPTER II.

CHAPTER III.

CHAPTER IV.

CHAPTER V.

CHAPTER VI.

CHAPTER VII.

CHAPTER VIII.

APPENDIX.

MEXICO UNDER MAXIMILIAN.

CHAPTER I.

Mexico before the conquest—Mexico at the time of Cortez—Historical sketch of Mexico during the last forty years—A constant scene of anarchy and confusion—Deplorable condition of the country, and of the people, at the time of the French Intervention—Self-government in Mexico impossible, and why—Geographical sketch of modern Mexico—Vast extent of the country—How the French intervention might have been prevented by the United States—Mr. McLane's treaty—Why it was not ratified.

WHEN Cortez landed in Mexico, a hundred years before the Puritans jumped ashore at Plymouth Rock, he found a people with an established government, skilled in useful arts, contented, hospitable, and courteous. They had no written literature, and consequently no written history. But in their sculpture, their mounds, their monuments, and their vast pyramids, were found recorded the annals of a former empire of barbaric and extravagant splendor. Even at this time, the Spaniards found around them in abundance, gold, silver, precious stones, woollen and cotton cloth, dyes of the most gorgeous purple and scarlet hues; and their avarice soon tempted them to deeds of treachery, rapacity, and blood. The system of merciless oppression, extortion, and fraud, which then commenced, continued for three hundred years.

Cortez, however, transplanted to Mexico a Spanish civilization, which, gradually spreading over the whole land, has endured to the present time. "Under this Spanish regime, princely cities grew with amazing rapidity, with royal mansions, and richly substantial abodes. Cathedrals and convents—vast, massive, everlasting—endowed and adorned with unmeasured wealth, impressed and awed every neighborhood. '*Haciendas*,' the homes of country gentlemen, controlling the labor of thousands of '*peons*,' at a mere nominal expense, dotted the land at wide distances from each other, with castle piles to defy attacks of robbers, of armies, or of time. Roads and bridges, arches, culverts, aqueducts and viaducts were built, master-pieces of skill and strength which still exist to attract the admiration and amazement of future ages. Argosies of silver, gold, ornamental woods, dyes, and drugs, floated off to old Spain. All the surface of the country was parcelled out, by royal grant, to favorites of fortune and the Crown. While one class surrendered themselves to aggrandizement, to high living, culture, politeness, elegance, and vice; the other was degraded into uncared-for pieces of machinery, of muscle, and bone. The whole country regarded but as 'the mine and mint' of Spain, its *agriculture* was not only *neglected,* but positively repressed by declaring *titheable* its natural luxuriant productions; treated as a *colony* of vassals, these were not allowed to be devoted to any of those branches of industry that foster the independent and manly growth of a people, but solely to those that would crush out whatever there might be of native aspiration; all ground down into one intense work of digging, separating, and coining silver and gold; and with the colonization of other peoples prevented, the exclusive Spaniards grafted themselves upon the conquered and debased aborigines, and the mongrel blood, with the haughtiness of the one side, and the indifference of the other glided into the life of the robber-guerilla, with the effect of perpetuating the exclusion of other races and the non-production of the country.

"Such is a brief history and outlined picture of Mexico from 'the conquest' down to the 'Independence' of 1821; such the unpromising elements for the foundation of an independent political society!"*

It would weary the reader without profit, to recount the incessant revolutions since 1821. In the space of forty-two years, down to 1863, Mexico

* Dr. Massey's lecture on Mexico.

was blessed, (or cursed) with thirty different forms of government, and with seventy-five different Presidents, Dictators, and other rulers.

First, however, Iturbide was proclaimed and crowned Emperor: and the empire of Mexico was formally recognized by President Monroe. Victoria the first President, was succeeded by Pedraza, " who was declared successful by a majority of only two votes over his competitor, Guerrero. *Before* Pedraza had taken his seat, he was 'pronounced' against by the defeated candidate, who in the course of the year, was successful, and Guerrero was 'declared' *legally* elected, with Bustamente for Vice-President. Guerrero had scarcely been installed when the Vice-President 'pronounced;' and Guerrero was overthrown, fled, caught, and *executed for treason,* and Bustamente installed as *President!* But very brief tranquillity followed, and Santa Anna 'pronounced' against Bustamente and in favor of Pedraza, whom he had been instrumental in driving out only two years before! Bustamente abdicated, and Pedraza was brought back to serve out the remaining three months of the term for which he had been declared first elected, in order that, upon the expiration of that brief period, Santa Anna might thus, dexterously, become his successor. This accomplished, in order to pay back a very natural grudge, when Santa Anna had gone up *after the Texans,* Bustamente took the opportunity again to usurp power.

"But it would be a waste of time to even sketch any more of these usurpations and overthrows, distinguished from each other scarcely by the respective pretences or plans of execution. At one time the 'Leperos,' the extreme of the degraded of that population, after sacking the capital and perpetrating every enormity and outrage, became 'the ruling class;' and Alvarez, with five thousand 'Pintos' —the Indians of the State of *Guerrero,* whose skins are spotted and eyes white with an hereditary leprosy peculiar to their mountains—in rags and filth, captured the city of Mexico, and 'declared' their chief President. Alvarez served less than three months, when, wearied of so much *civilization,* he voluntarily and arbitrarily turned over the government to Comonfort, and betook himself to his own kind, in their own mountain passes, where he still *reigns!*

"The ease with which the supreme authority could be destroyed or overthrown; the absurd facility with which constitutions and so-called constitutional elections could be created or set aside by any bold and daring chieftain, had been established in the first months of 'independent' existence; and experience has shown how many there were to take advantage of the example.

"The part played by the condition of 'the Public Treasury' can have no stronger illustration than in the fact that Herrera, fortifying his exchequer with the United States gold which bought the 'peace' of 1848, held on to the Presidency for the whole term for which he had been selected—the only example in history since the first Presidency."*

Up to the year 1836, the territorial extent of Mexico was twice as great as at present. It included Texas and California, New Mexico, Utah, and Arizona. At the end of the Texan revolution, in 1836, and when Texas became finally separated from Mexico in 1837, the limits of that state were not accurately ascertained, and the question remained in dispute until the annexation of Texas to the United States in 1845. The annexation was followed by the war with Mexico in 1846 and 1847. In 1848, when peace was made, we had "acquired" a generous slice of Mexico, including what is now California, Utah, Nevada, Colorado, Arizona, and New Mexico. Shorn of these States and of Texas, Mexico still remained, however, a country of vast extent. It stretches now through sixteen degrees of latitude, from the sixteenth to the thirty-second, or as far as from Portland in Maine, to New Orleans; and without counting Yucatan at all, through twenty-five degrees of longitude, from the fourteenth to the

* Dr. Massey's lecture on Mexico.

fortieth degree of west longitude, or many miles further than from Boston to St. Louis. From the north-west corner of Mexico to the city of Chiapas, south of the Gulf of Campeachy, the distance is one thousand nine hundred miles, while from Portland in Maine to Galveston in Texas, it is only one thousand seven hundred. From El Paso to the city of Mexico the distance is one thousand miles; as far as from St. Louis to Hartford in Connecticut, or from Baltimore to New Orleans.

The territory of Mexico contains seven hundred and ninety three thousand square miles, or more than the following twenty-four states in our own country, namely:

Virginia	contains	61,300	sq.	miles.
Florida	"	59,200	"	"
Georgia	"	58,000	"	"
Michigan	"	56,200	"	"
Alabama	"	50,700	"	"
Mississippi	"	47,100	"	"
Wisconsin	"	53,900	"	"
New York	"	46,000	"	"
Pennsylvania	"	46,000	"	"
Tennessee	"	45,600	"	"
North Carolina	"	45,000	"	"
Ohio	"	39,900	"	"
Kentucky	"	37,700	"	"
Indiana	"	33,700	"	"

Maine	contains	30,000	sq.	miles
South Carolina	"	24,500	"	"
Maryland	"	9,300	"	"
New Jersey...............	"	8,300	"	"
New Hampshire and Vermont.	"	18,200	"	"
Massachusetts and Connecticut	"	12,400	"	"
Delaware and Rhode Island ...	"	3,300	"	"
Total		786,400	sq.	miles.

The above States all lie together, and it will be well to give a look at them on the map. They comprise the whole of that part of the territory of the United States which lies east of the Mississippi river. Let us glance now, at the extent of the twenty-eight Mexican States, as follows:—

STATES, CAPITALS, AND POPULATION OF MEXICO.

Mexico is divided into twenty-two States, six Territories, and a Federal District.*

* The Constitution of 1857, made in this political division of Mexico the following alterations:

TITLE II.—SECTION 2. ART. 43. The Mexican confederation is composed of twenty-four States and one Territory, the names of which are as follows: Aguascalientes, Colima, Chiapa, Chihuahua, Durango, Guanajuato, Guerrero, Jalisco, Mexico, Michoacan, Nuevo Leon and Cohahuila, Oajaca, Puebla, Queretaro, San Luis Potosi, Sinaloa, Sonora, Tabasco, Tamaulipas, Tlaxcala, the Valley of Mexico, Vera Cruz, Yucatan, Zacatecas, and the Territory of Lower California.

ART. 44. The States of Aguascalientes, Chiapa, Chihuahua,

States.	Superficial or square miles.	Population in 1858.	Capitals.	Inhabitants.
Aguascalientes	2,739	88,329	Aguascalientes	39,693
Chiapa	18,679	167,472	San Cristobal	7,649
Chihuahua	83,512	164,073	Chihuahua	12,069
Cohahuila	36,572	67,590	Saltillo	19,898
Durango	48,489	144,331	Durango	22,000
Guanajuato	11,396	729,103	Guanajuato	48,954
Guerrero	32,003	279,109	Tixtla	6,501
Jalisco	48,591	804,058	Guadalajara	68,000
Mexico	19,539	1,129,629	Toluca	12,000
Michoacan	22,993	554,585	Morelia	25,000
Nuevo Leon	16,688	145,779	Monterey	17,309
Oajaca	23,642	525,938	Oajaca	25,000
Puebla	8,879	658,609	Puebla	71,631
Queretaro	1,884	165,155	Queretaro	29,702
San Luis Potosi	28,142	397,189	San Luis Potosi	19,678
Sinaloa	33,722	163,714	Caliacan	9,647
Sonora	100,228	139,374	Ures	6,009

Durango, Guerrero, Mexico, Puebla, Queretaro, Sinaloa, Sonora, Tamaulipas, and the Territory of Lower California, retain the boundaries which they have had hitherto (1857.)

Art. 45. The States of Colima and of Tlaxcala retain, being erected into States, boundaries which they had when they were only Territories of the confederacy.

Art. 46. The State of the Valley of Mexico comprises the territory which has, until now, (1857,) formed the federal district; but it will only take rank as a State when the federal government shall have been removed to some other place.

Art. 47. The State of Nuevo Leon and Cohahuila, comprises the former Territory of Nuevo Leon and Cohahuila, unless the hacienda of Bonanza shall be re-incorporated into the State of Zacatecas.

The other States, Guanajuato, Jalisco, Vera Cruz, and San Luis Potosi, make some exchanges of towns to rectify their frontier lines.

States.	Superficial or Square miles.	Population in 1858.	Capitals.	Inhabitants.
Tabasco...............	12,359	70,628	San Juan Bautista.	5,300
Tamaulipas.........	30,344	109,673	Victoria...............	4,621
Vera Cruz...........	27,415	349,125	Vera Cruz	9,647
Yucatan	48,869	668,623	Merida..................	23,575
Zacatecas.............	27,768	296,789	Zacatecas	15,427
Territories.				
Lower California..	60,662	12,000	La Paz	1,254
Colima	3,019	62,109	Colima..................	31,774
Isla de Carman....	7,298	11,807	V. del Carmen	3,068
Sierra Gorda........	3,127	55,358	San Luis de la Paz.	4,411
Tehuantepec	12,526	82,395	Minatitlan............	339
Tlaxcala	1,984	90,158	Tlaxcala...............	3,463
District.				
Federal District...	90	260,534	City of Mexico.....	205,000
Total.........	793,179	8,400,236		

The population has increased since 1793 at the following rate:

Years.	Population.	Years.	Population.
1793	5,273,029	1839	7,065,000
1803	5,873,100	1842	7,015,509
1808	6,500,000	1851	7,867,520
1824	6,500,000	1854	7,853,395
1830	7,996,000	1858	8,287,413

The population is composed of about one million white, descendants of Europeans, four million Indians, six thousand blacks, and three million four hundred thousand metis (part white and part Indian) or mulattoes (part white and part black.) The foreigners, to the number of nine thousand two hundred and thirty-four in 1838, are classed as follows: Spaniards, five thousand one hundred and forty-one; French, two thousand

and forty-eight; English, six hundred and fifteen; Germans, six hundard and eighty-one; Americans, four hundred and forty-four; miscellaneous, four hundred and five.

In 1856, the Mexican people rose against Santa Anna, and made M. Comonfort President. Quarrels between the "republican" chiefs, however, immediately ensued. Sixteen days after he had been inaugurated, Comonfort felt it necessary to arrest Benito Juarez, in order to prevent the latter from seizing the supreme power. On the 11th of January, 1858, however, the latter was released. He immediately set up the standard of revolt, and on the 22d of the same month, he overthrew the administration of Comonfort, and proclaimed himself President of Mexico.

In 1860, the Governments of England, France, and Spain made a simultaneous demand upon Mexico, for the settlement of certain claims of long standing due to the citizens of those countries. The Mexican treasury, of course, was empty as usual. Juarez could not pay these claims, which amounted to forty million dollars. The three nations had anticipated this inability. They sent a combined fleet and an allied army, and this allied force appeared off Vera Cruz in December, 1861. This was the commencement of the French intervention in Mexico.

Before this, however, certain American statesmen had endeavored to make two treaties with Mexico,

The first was negotiated by Mr. McLane, in Mr. Buchanan's administration, in 1860.

That treaty would have been vastly advantageous to us in a commercial point of view, and would, in all probability, have prevented the subsequent intervention by England and France, and the present establishment of the Mexican Empire.

By this treaty the Mexican Government granted the right of way for railroad purposes, through the States of Sonora and Chihuahua, with a protectorate over the same; in consideration of which the United States agreed to loan Juarez four millions of dollars. What would have been the result of the ratification of this treaty? In the first place, it would have firmly established the constitutional republican government of Mexico, under President Juarez. It would have enabled the latter to have paid off the foreign debts of Mexico, thus taking away all pretence for subsequent French interference; and, finally, it would have enabled the Mexican people to demonstrate whether or not they were capable of living under a Republican Government. Besides that, it would have given us an opportunity, and the means of building a Southern Pacific Railroad, running through Texas, with its western terminus at the seaport of Guaymas. Suppose the four million dollars had never been repaid, what then? We would have a protectorate over the whole of the two northern States of Mexico.

They would already be in our possession, and they would, ultimately, have been ceded to the United States.

WHY WAS THE TREATY NOT RATIFIED.

That treaty, however, failed to receive the ratification of the Senate. It is true that this treaty pledged the United States to uphold the Monroe doctrine (as it was then understood, and as it has been until now understood) in Mexico. Was that the reason why it was not ratified? Whatever the reason was, the refusal of the Senate to ratify this treaty, prepared the way for the downfall of the Mexican Republic, and opened the way for the establishment of the empire.

Mr. Buchanan, under whose administration this treaty was negotiated, thus speaks of it:—

"The President having failed in obtaining authority from Congress to employ a military force in Mexico, as a last resort adopted the policy of concluding a treaty with the Constitutional Government. By this means he thought something might be accomplished, both to satisfy the long-deferred claims of American citizens, and to prevent foreign interference with the internal Government of Mexico. Accordingly, Mr. McLane, on the 14th day of December, 1859, signed a 'treaty of transit and commerce' with the Mexican Republic, and also a 'convention to enforce treaty stipulations, and to maintain order and security in the territory of the republics of Mexico and the United States.' These treaties secured peculiar and highly valuable advantages to our trade and commerce, especially in articles the production of our agriculture and manufactures. They also guaranteed to us the secure possession of the Tehuantepec route, and of several other transit routes for our commerce, free from duty, across the territories of the republic, on its way to California and our other possessions on the northwest coast, as well as to the independent republics on the Pacific coast and in eastern Asia.

"In consideration of these advantages, and in compensation for the revenue surrendered by Mexico on the goods and merchandize transported free of duty through the territory of that republic, the Government of the United States agreed to pay the Government of Mexico the sum of four millions of dollars.' Of this sum two millions were to be paid immediately to Mexico, and the remaining two millions were to be retained by our Government 'for the payment of the claims of citizens of the United States against the Government of the Republic of Mexico for injuries already inflicted, and which may be proven to be just, according to the law and usages of nations and the principles of equity.' It was believed that these stipulations, whilst providing two millions toward the payment of the claims of our citizens, would enable President Juarez, with the remaining two millions, to expel the usurping Government of Miramon from the capital, and place the Constitutional Government in possession of the whole territory of the

Republic. This, we need not say, would greatly promote the interests of the United States. Besides, what was vastly important, these treaties, by vesting in the United States territorial and commercial rights which we would be bound to defend, might for this reason have prevented any European Government from attempting to acquire dominion over the territories of Mexico, and thus the Monroe doctrine would probably have remained inviolate. With this view Mr. McLane was seriously impressed. In his dispatch of September 14, 1859, to the Secretary of State, communicating the treaties, he expressed the apprehension that, should they not be ratified, further anarchy would prevail in Mexico, until it should be terminated by direct interference from some other quarter.

On the 4th of January, 1860, the President submitted to the Senate the treaty and the convention, with a view to their ratification, together with the dispatch of Mr. McLane. These, on the same day, were referred to the Committee on Foreign Relations. Whether any or what other proceedings were had in relation to them we are unable to state, the injunction of secresy never having been removed by the Senate. Mr. McLane, who was then in Washington, had a conference with the committee, and received the impression that a comparative unanimity existed in favor of the principal provisions of the treaty; but in regard to the convention, the contingency of its possible abuse was referred to as constituting an objection to its ratification. Certain it is that neither the one nor the other was ever approved by the Senate, and consequently both became a dead letter. The Republic of Mexico was thus left to its fate, and has since become an empire under the dominion of a scion of the House of Hapsburg, protected by the Emperor of the French. The righteous claims of American citizens have therefore been indefinitely postponed.

CHAPTER II.

How the Mexican Empire came to be Established—Origin of the French Intervention—The United States had "Conquered and Divided" Mexico, and then Left it to its Fate—Touching Appeal of the Gentlemen of Mexico to the United States Government—Its Rejection—They Appeal, as a Last Resort, to the Emperor Napoleon—Landing of the French Army at Vera Cruz—Military Operations—Capture of Puebla—The French Army Enters the City of Mexico—The Emperor's Instructions to General Forey—Contrast between our Treatment of Mexico in 1847, and the Treatment of Mexico by Napoleon—Convocation of the Assembly of Notables—Their Address to the Mexican Nation—General Forey Returns to France—He is Succeeded by General Bazaine.

SUCH was the deplorable condition of Mexico, when the Emperor Napoleon determined to deliver that unhappy country from anarchy, and give her a permanent government. France had had claims of long standing against Mexico, of which it had been impossible to obtain a settlement, owing to the absence of any permanent government with which to treat. When France made war against Mexico, in 1861, what she required was, the redress of grievances and a government able and willing to give guarantees for the future. That was certainly not more than *we* had required of Mexico, when we made war against her in 1846. We required ample indemnity for the past, which we took in the shape of nearly a quarter of her territory; and security for the future, which we got by reducing her to a position of utter helplessness. We had got all that we cared for from Mexico, when we "acquired" California, Arizona, Utah, Colorado, and New Mexico, in 1848; and we then left that country to her fate.

Ten years elapsed, and the condition of the country became more and more deplorable. Then, in 1859, the intelligent portion of the people of Mexico made one last effort for the establishment of some form of government that would guarantee public order and private interests. There was a prospect, at one time, that this would be accomplished by direct treaty with the United States—the treaty negotiated by Mr. McLane.

The publication of that treaty, with the accompanying correspondence, revealed the fact that no government existing or likely to exist in Mexico had the power to give effect to treaty stipulations, or protection to the citizens of the United States sojourning in Mexico. The accompanying convention provided for the direct intervention of the military power of the United States to enable the Mexican Government to insure the due execution of the commercial treaty, and to secure the safety of the transits conceded by the same.

This treaty, as well as the subsequent one negotiated by Mr. Corwin for the same purpose, failed to receive the ratification of the United States Senate; and it is not too much to say that the extinction of the Mexican Republic is the result of the failure of those treaties. The Mexicans who, in 1863, invited Maximilian to the throne, before applying for help in Europe, having failed in securing the intervention of the United States Government in their behalf, "raised a large fund," says Mr. Sylvester Mowry, "and proposed to certain influential and intelligent gentlemen in the United States to unite with them in establishing in Mexico a strong government. Several officers of the old regular army were enlisted in the cause, some of them now distinguished and dear to the American people. The arrangements were being perfected; a government with probably Iturbide at its head was to have been established—with the administration of affairs in American hands. Money to an adequate amount to secure success was obtained—eight millions alone from Mexico. A memoir prepared by one of the leading men of New York to-day, assisted by McClellan, Charles P. Stone, the writer, and the most intelligent, wealthy, and influential Mexicans, which, I am informed, has been perused with great pleasure and profit by the Emperor Napoleon, embodied the statistics and plan of the enterprise. When success was certain if let alone, the United States Government, whose neutrality was implored by all worth recognizing in Mexico, put out the hand of authority, and the enterprise was reluctantly abandoned. Failing in getting either private or public assistance here, the Mexicans, who had property and life at stake, appealed to Europe, and the throne of Maximilian is the result."

Subsequently, one of these Mexican gentlemen said to Mr. Mowry:

"We tried, as you know, for years to get the United States to help Mexico. She would neither do it as a government nor permit an association of private individuals to do it. As a last hope, we came to Europe, and got the help we needed. If the United States will recognize Maximilian, or say that they will remain neutral, and keep so, we can get all the money in Europe needed for our government until the home revenues are sufficient to sustain it and pay the interest on our national debt. If the United States makes war on Maximilian she makes war on Mexico. Europe will furnish us money and men, and we, the gentlemen of Mexico, will gain in the army at least the glory of dying for our country, in defence of the only government worthy the name it has had or can hope to have."

This was the simple, truthful sentiment of the intelligent, wealthy, decent, responsible people of Mexico.

The French forces landed at Vera Cruz in December, 1861. The whole of the year 1862 passed away without any serious movement being made by the Emperor Napoleon for the conquest of Mexico. His army was on the spot, making demonstrations toward Puebla but it would seem that he was waiting to see whether our government would take any step to uphold the Monroe doctrine. No obstacle was placed in his way by our government, however, and on the 19th of November, 1862, Mr. Corwin wrote to Mr. Seward that there were then forty-two thousand French troops besieging Puebla, and that the capture of the city of Mexico itself would speedily follow that of Puebla. On the 27th of January, 1863, there were twenty thousand Mexican troops defending Puebla, which was strongly fortified; while on the 1st of May, 1863, General Comonfort, with fifteen thousand additional Mexican troops, was advancing to the relief of the place. Before the end of May, however, Comonfort was defeated, and Puebla was captured by the French. Early in June, 1863, Juarez evacuated the city of Mexico, and on the 12th, General Forey entered and took possession of the capital.

This is the proper place to examine the instructions of the Emperor Napoleon, under which these military operations were conducted. They are contained in his letter to General Forey, as follows:

"THE EMPEROR TO GENERAL FOREY.

"FONTAINEBLEAU, *July* 3, 1862.

"MY DEAR GENERAL:—At the moment when you are about to leave for Mexico, charged with political and military powers, I deem it useful that you should understand my wishes.

"This is the line of conduct which you are expected to pursue: 1. To issue a proclamation on your arrival, the principal ideas of which will be indicated to you. 2. To receive with the greatest kindness all Mexicans who may join you. 3. To espouse the quarrel of no party, but to announce that all is provisional until the Mexican nation shall have declared its wishes; to show a great respect for religion, but to reassure at the same time the holders of national property. 4. To supply, pay, and arm, according to your ability, the auxiliary Mexican troops: to give them the chief part in combats. 5. To maintain among your troops, as well as among the auxiliaries, the most severe discipline; to repress with vigor every act, every design, which might wound the Mexicans, for their pride of character must not be forgotten, and it is of the first importance to the success of the undertaking to conciliate the good will of the people.

"When we shall have reached the city of Mexico, it is desirable that you should have an understanding with the notable persons of every shade of opinion who shall have espoused our cause, in order to organize a provisional government. This government will submit to the Mexican people the question of the form of political rule which shall be definitively established. An assembly will be afterward elected in accordance with the Mexican laws.

"You will aid the new government to introduce into the administration of affairs, and especially into the finances, that regularity of which France offers the best example. To effect this, persons will be sent thither capable of aiding this new organization.

"The end to be attained is not to impose upon the Mexicans a form of government which will be distasteful to them, but to aid them to establish, in conformity with their wishes, a government which may have some chance of stability, and will assure to France the redress of the wrongs of which she complains.

"It is not to be denied that if they prefer a monarchy it is in the interest of France to aid them in this path.

"Persons will not be wanting who will ask you why we propose to spend men and money to establish a regular government in Mexico.

"In the present state of the world's civilization Europe is not indifferent to the prosperity of America; for it is she which nourishes our industry and gives life to our commerce. It is our interest that the Republic of the United States shall be powerful and prosperous, but it is not at all to our interest that she should grasp the whole Gulf of Mexico, rule thence the Antilles as well as South America, and be the sole dispenser of the products of the New World. We see to-day, by sad experience, how precarious is the fate of an industry which is forced to seek its raw material in a single market, under all the vicissitudes to which that market is subject.

"If, on the contrary, Mexico preserve its independence, and maintain the integrity of its territory, if a stable government be there established with the aid of

France, we shall have restored to the Latin race on the other side of the ocean its force and its prestige; we shall have guaranteed the safety of our own and the Spanish colonies in the Antilles. We shall have established our benign influence in the centre of America, and this influence, while creating immense outlets for our commerce, will procure the raw material which is indispensable to our industry.

"Mexico, thus regenerated, will always be favorable to us, not only from gratitude, but also because her interests will be identical with our own, and because she will find a support in the good will of European powers.

"To-day, therefore, our military honor involved, the demands of our policy, the interest of our industry and our commerce, all impose upon us the duty of marching upon Mexico, there boldly planting our flag, and establishing perhaps a monarchy, if not incompatible with the national sentiment of the country, but at least a government which will promise some stability.

"NAPOLEON."

These admirable instructions were faithfully carried out. On the 12th of June, 1863, the French army, under General Forey, entered the city of Mexico as conquerors, precisely the same as the American army, under General Scott, had entered that capital in 1847. At that time, and in 1848, the good citizens of Mexico, the men of wealth, of property, and of education, implored General

Scott to remain, and give them a good government. They wished to put themselves under the protection of the United States government, and offered to do so. The United States government laughed at them. They cut off a generous slice of the country, including the whole of California, Utah, New Mexico, Arizona, Colorado, etc., and left the rest of Mexico to her fate. The eleven years of anarchy followed, from 1849 to 1860.

Now let the reader observe how differently Napoleon treated the country. He had, in 1863, the same right that we had, in 1847, to seize upon three or four rich Mexican States, and make French provinces of them. Did he do so? No. Let us observe what he did do.

On the 16th of June, 1863, General Forey, after consultation with the French minister residing in Mexico, called together thirty-five of the most eminent citizens of the country, men distinguished both for their abilities and their virtues, and deliberated with them in regard to the state of the country. These gentlemen were men acquainted with everybody of note or prominence in the whole country. It was agreed that they should designate two hundred and fifteen Mexican citizens, from the various States, constituting, with themselves, an Assembly of Notables, to whom should be intrusted the duty of determining upon the form of government to be adopted.

The supreme executive power being vested temporarily in three eminent Mexican citizens, Messrs. Almonte, Salas, and Ormaechea, they issued, on the 24th of June, 1863, the following manifesto to the Mexican nation:

"MANIFESTO OF THE SUPREME EXECUTIVE POWER TO THE NATION.

"MEXICANS:—Having been appointed by the superior committee of government, to exercise the supreme powers of the nation, it is right that we should instruct you of the very grave situation in which we find ourselves, and of our designs in fulfilling the mighty charge that we have received.

"Never was the Mexican nation seen with more misfortunes nor with more solid hopes. A disciplined and courageous army, a great and civilized power, have undertaken to save us from the unfathomable abyss of evils to which, as blindly as impiously, a misled minority of our countrymen have brought us. They labor for our national restoration not by the terror of arms, nor by anti-social principles.

"The force that comes to protect us will only be used to conquer that which persists in destroying us; to the errors which have perverted us there will be opposed the truths that regenerate nations; to the demoralization which has overturned every thing there will be applied the justice which maintains the order of nations.

"We know how many sophisms and calumnies those

who have persisted in our ruin have employed and employ to diffuse among you aversion or mistrust with respect to the intervention. Compare their sophisms with the facts which you behold; their calumnies with the conduct which is observed; their insidious promises with the evidence of the disasters and desolation that you contemplate. Compare the deeds with the words of the magnanimous and enlightened Emperor: No hostility to the nation, and sufficient mildness even toward those who compromise it and tyrannize over it.

"Driving from the capital the power which the pretended constitution of 1857 systematized in evil, by evil, and for evil, the representatives of the Emperor have made no delay in establishing the provisional Mexican government, which will govern until the nation, more amply represented, shall fix freely and definitely the form of government which Mexicans ought to have permanently. The chimeras of conquest with which it was attempted to alarm the thoughtless are made evident and vanish. Mexico has again self-government, and is able and at liberty to choose, among all the political institutions, that which suits it best, and has the most glorious titles and firmest guarantees of stability.

"In the mean time it is incumbent upon us to govern *ad interim* this suffering and disorganized nation; a task immensely arduous and complicated, and much superior to our strength. Can we, in our transitory administration, repair the disorders and injuries of half a century? That which was founded by three centuries of peace, and a gradual progress, is not restored in a few days; we can only aspire to take the road and guide you in the first steps. No doubt Divine Providence reserves to more competent persons the consummating all the moral, social, political, and industrial restoration of Mexico.

"The work is grand, and will be the sooner realized according as your co-operation is decided and general. We shall do very little if just men of all classes, parties, and ranks of our society do not aid our intentions in their respective spheres.

"We behold you vacillating and uncertain about the future of our beloved country, as dejected with cares and anxieties, as fearful of new misfortunes, anxious for peace, and distrustful of provoking new wars; ruined and panting for tranquillity to restore your fortunes, with aversion for the political and administrative theories which we have tried, and jealous of trying other new ones. Order and disorder, misery and prosperity, conciliation and discord, are at your choice. You have two powers in view—one whose long tyranny and bad passions you have so wofully experienced, and another whose measured and just behavior you are able to observe: the one which is not satisfied with all your treasures, nor with your most necessary furniture, and the other which commences by relieving you of taxes, and introducing the severest economy: the one which fled from this city without any other support than the faction whose illegitimate interests it foments, and the other which, solidly fixed in Europe, will rest upon the legitimate interest and cardinal principles of society: that, in short, which, sacrificing to personal interest, or that of party, all that was orderly, just, useful, respectable, and sacred, brought our country to wars, and this, which, by the light and unconquered force of Catholicism, according to the invincible rules of good government, and supported by the bountiful protection of France, omitted nothing, that Mexico may rise in the New World, as vigorous, enlightened, and improved as corresponds to the admirable abundance of her elements of prosperity.

"Very grave affairs are about to occupy our attention. Peace, which has its roots only in justice and well-defined liberty; agriculture, now so decayed, the basis of every kind of industry, and which, for so long, has been the comman prey of revolutionists and highwaymen; commerce, so paralyzed and fallen, from the public insecurity in the country; mining, a first-rate branch of industry, in decay from the prejudices and special burden which it has suffered; the unmeasured exactions in the towns and the demoralization in agreements; the arts either destroyed or impoverished; the administration of justice, with some honorable exceptions, so corrupt and tardy; security on the highways or in the inhabited places altogether lost; the vagrancy of all classes and ranks serving as a food for disorder and national depravation; finally, the reparation of the moral and physical disasters made by the so-called system of liberty and reform, for which the two powers will co-operate together as far as concerns them, united or separate, and the tribunals in cases within their competency.

"The well-deserving army will likewise merit a preferable attention, and their sufferings will be taken into consideration, proceeding, without delay, to its reorganization. The worthy mutilated of the national independence will not be forgotten, nor less the suffering widows of the honored soldiers who have died in defence of their country.

"The Catholic religion is re-established and free. The church will exercise its authority without having an enemy in the government, and the State will concert with it the manner of resolving the grave questions which are pendant.

"The atheism which has been planted in the establishments of instruction, and the infamous propaganda of immoral doctrines which have ruined us, must cease. Catholic instruction, solid and of the greatest possible extent, and new literary careers and guarantees for good teachers, will be the object of our labors.

"We have still to get rid of the so-called constitutional government, which is only able and only knows to do evil, which courts no good in its career of innovations and destruction. Whilst it exists, we Mexicans shall have no peace, nor our fortunes security, nor commerce increase. The Franco-Mexican army will, as the first act they perform, pursue it until it surrenders or is driven from the national territory, and in proportion as the towns shake off their intolerable yoke, they will begin to feel the repose and prosperity which the people already liberated enjoy. At the same time suitable measures will be dictated to expedite the pacification of the departments, and diminish the ruin which the agents of demagogism still occasion them.

"Our misdeeds, and the acts committed by terrorists against friendly nations, have discredited us in the Old World. Good and dignified relations will be opened again with injured governments and with the Sovereign Pontiff; every effort will be made to ratify the obligations of Mexico with friendly powers, and with the protection of France and the other nations that shall support the new government, we shall be respected abroad, and the honor and credit of the nation will be repaired.

"We have told you frankly what we think of the new situation, and what we intend to do in the difficult commission which we have received, in spite of our insufficiency. Much will be done if eminent men of all kinds assist. Let our disgraceful discord at last end. Let the scandal which we have given to the world cease. Let there be concord, union, peace, and public spirit among us. Let the sordid speculations at public misfortunes be extirpated, and let those riches be turned to great and lucrative industrial enterprises. Let honest labor be the foundation of fortunes; let functionaries have no power over the laws, nor the laws over morality. Let religion and authority, property and liberty, order and peace, be at last precious realities for Mexicans. May the God of armies, who has so directly favored our cause, reward the generosity and sincere intervention of France, and the patriotic intention with which we good Mexicans have accepted it, with the speedy grandeur and prosperity of the nation.

"Palace of the supreme executive power in Mexico, the 24th of June, 1863.

"JUAN N. ALMONTE.
"JOSE MARIANO SALAS.
"JUAN B. ORMAECHEA."

Having thus terminated the great mission which had been intrusted to him, General Forey returned to France. He was succeeded in command of the French army in Mexico by General Bazaine, to whom, on the 17th of August, 1863, the Emperor Napoleon sent the following letter of instructions:

CHAPTER III.

The Emperor's Instructions to General Bazaine—Proceedings of the Assembly of Notables—They Determine upon a Limited Monarchy, and Offer the Crown of Mexico to Prince Maximilian—A Deputation of the Notables Proceeds to Europe—Offer of the Crown to Maximilian—Remarkable Reply of Prince Maximilian to the Offer of the Crown—The Conditions upon which he Bases his Consent—Approval of these Conditions by the Emperor Napoleon.

THE EMPEROR'S INSTRUCTIONS TO MARSHAL BAZAINE.

"PARIS, *August* 17, 1863.

"GENERAL:—At the moment in which you find yourself invested with the plenitude of political and military power, and when, thanks to the heroism of our soldiers and the skill of our chiefs, the elaboration of a new political regime supersedes the clash of arms in Mexico, I deem it useful to retrace once more the ideas with which the Emperor's government is inspired. Those ideas have been clearly indicated in the letter addressed by his majesty to General Forey, July 3, 1862, and to this memorable document we must always refer.

"I shall not return to enumerate the facts which caused our intervention, or the incidents, too well known, which have signalized the first phase of it, whilst we were engaged in collective action with other powers. I refer to them merely to call to mind the fact that, left alone, we have used our independence only to pursue the work which it was not in our power to accomplish in conjunction with the rest, and without deviating from the line which, from the beginning, we had traced out for ourselves, and which we had indicated to our allies. In acting thus, we believe that we serve the general interests of Europe.

"We have recognized that the legitimacy of our intervention resulted solely from our grievances against the government of that country; we have declared that, whatever rights war conferred on us, we sought neither conquest nor colonial establishment, nor even any political or commercial advantage to the exclusion of other powers. Penetrated, however, with the idea, which several onerous experiences justified, that an expedition, analogous to those of which the traditional proceedings of the Mexican Government have so often imposed on us and others the necessity, would assure us only very precarious satisfaction and no guarantees for the future, we have thought that it would be worthy of us and profitable for all to remind the Mexican people of the iniquities of their government, and to afford them, if they desired to avail themselves of it, the occasion and the means to react against the elements of dissolution accumulated on their soil by a deplorable succession of anarchical powers. We applaud ourselves heartily now for not having despaired of the good sense and patriotism of the Mexican nation. For the rest, we most unequivocally eschew, as you are aware, any intention of substituting our influence in place of the free resolutions of the country; we promise it our moral support to second whatever efforts it may wish to make in its own independence; but it is from its own loins that its regeneration must issue.

"We have received with pleasure, as a symptom of favorable augury, the manifestation of the Assembly of Notables of Mexico in favor of the establishment of a monarchy, and the name of the prince called to the empire. However, as I have indicated to you in a preceding dispatch, *we can consider the votes of the Assembly at Mexico only as the first indication of the disposition of the country.* With all the authority which attaches to the eminent men who compose it, the Assembly recommends to its fellow-countrymen the adoption of monarchical institutions, and it designates a prince for their suffrages. It belongs, however, to the provisional government to collect those suffrages in such a manner as to banish all doubt in regard to the expression of the will of the country. It is not my part to indicate to you the mode to be adopted in order that this indispensable result should be completely attained; we must search for this in the local customs and institutions. Whether the municipalities should be called upon to declare their wishes in the different provinces according as they shall have recovered the free disposal of themselves, or whether the lists should be opened by their care in order to collect the votes, the best method will be that which shall insure the largest manifestation of the popular will in all its independence and sincerity. General, the Emperor particularly recommends this essential point to your most careful attention.

"Other questions at the same time demand your solicitude. We have flattered ourselves with the idea that we represent in Mexico the cause of progress and of civilization, and our regard for our responsibility does not permit us to accept the species of provisional guardianship with which we are invested by circumstances, except on condition of serving that cause faithfully by our counsels and by our actions. From this point of view, we have to regret certain measures which contrast in an unfavorable manner with the ideas which we ought to strive to establish. Sequestrations, prohibitions, outlawries, have too often been, in Mexico, the arms used by parties in straits, in their desperate contests—too often, indeed, not to interdict the use of them to a government that goes to conserve and restore. Adopted, doubtless, in view of the urgent necessities of which I cannot judge, they can have but a provisional character, and at the moment at which I write to you they are certainly revoked, if they have not been already so at the reception of the instructions sent out by the last packet.

"The reorganization of the Mexican army is one of the most important questions which should, at present, occupy the attention of the provisional government and yours. It is the duty of the minister of war to transmit special instructions to you on this point. I will confine myself to saying, that, the desire of the Emperor's government being to restrict, as promptly as circumstances will permit, the extent and the duration of our occupation, it is essential that this reorganization should be pushed forward with all possible activity, and that it is desirable that in future, and in proportion to the progress realized, an honorable share of duty should be assigned to the Mexican army. In the interest of the country and its ulterior development, as well as to provide for present necessities, I recommend you to press upon the government the duty of applying its utmost care to multiply the means of communication, and to assure, on the roads which now exist, security of transportation and rapid exchange of correspondence.

"Without directly substituting your initiative for that of the government, all your counsels, General, should tend to have the administration, properly so-called, reconstituted in conditions of regularity and strength, such as may give confidence to the country and reassure it against all ideas of reactionary and exclusive policy. Under the shadow of our flag, all parties can be worthily reconciled, and we will induce them to this; but as we repudiate their passions, we must never allow it to serve as a shelter for them to work out their revenges.

"The same principles should preside over the reorganization of the judicial administration, and you will have to recommend to the government, to be inspired with them in the choice of magistrates and in the impulse which it will give them, the independence and honesty of the magistracy being able to contribute powerfully to elevate the moral state of a people among whom the notions of right must have been very much blunted by the contact of so many revolutions.

"The existing administrative and judicial institutions appear, moreover, to answer the wants and customs of the country. Your counsels should, therefore, be directed, in this regard, rather to the choice of functionaries and the directions to be impressed upon them, than to the institutions themselves.

"It is not entirely so with regard to the finances. We have there, moreover, a direct interest, which commands us to watch more closely over the execution of such regulations as ought to assure to the country the benefits of a regular system of accountability. The proper management of the public money is the guarantee of our debts, and, from this point of view, we have good reason to exercise an active control over the financial administration. We have, for the rest, as far as depended on us, facilitated its reorganization by assuring to it the precious support of special agents delegated for that purpose by the minister of finance. Under their enlightened influence, the germs of prosperity, so varied and abundant, which the country possesses cannot fail to be rapidly developed.

"I have spoken of our claims. They are, as you know, General, of two kinds: those which are anterior to the war, and those which have their origin in the war. As to the former, they will be all referred for examination to a commission which shall be instituted in connection with my department, and which shall be composed in such a way as to assure an unquestionable authority to its decisions. The total amount to be presented to the Mexican Government will be composed of the sum of all these claims that shall be recognized by the commission as legitimately founded in justice.

"As to those which proceed from the war which we are now maintaining, my colleagues in the departments of war and marine are occupied in combining such elements as will allow them to form a proper estimate of the expenses of which we shall have to claim reimbursement. We shall most likely be able to transmit to you, by the next packet, the result of this labor, and you will then have to present to the provisional government for acceptance the demand for reimbursement of the sum which shall be indicated to you.

"DROUYN DE LHUYS."

The Assembly of Notables comprised the men who had, in 1848 and 1849, and again in 1860, implored the United States to save Mexico and give her a good government. Let the reader remember the experience they had had, of forty years of anarchy in Mexico, owing to the want of a good government. Let the efforts be remembered which they had made to establish a good government themselves, under the protection of the United States. Let it be remembered how all their efforts had failed, and how they and their country had been spurned by the United States, and the latter given up by us to continued anarchy.

But there was one great power that had not despised them; there was one powerful hand stretched out to save their country and to give them a good government. They were not fools, neither were they ungrateful. Here is their action:

"The provisional supreme executive power of the nation to the inhabitants thereof: Know ye that the Assembly of Notables has thought fit to decree as follows:

"'The Assembly of Notables, in virtue of the decree of the 16th ultimo, that it should make known the form of government which best suited the nation, in use of the full right which the nation has to constitute itself, and as its organ and interpreter, declares, with absolute liberty and independence, as follows:

"'1. The Mexican nation adopts as its form of government a limited hereditary monarchy, with a Catholic prince.

"'2. The sovereign shall take the title of Emperor of Mexico.

"'3. The imperial crown of Mexico is offered to his imperial and royal highness the Prince Ferdinand Maximilian, Archduke of Austria, for himself and his descendants.

"'4. If, under circumstances which cannot be foreseen, the Archduke of Austria, Ferdinand Maximilian, should not take possession of the throne which is offered to him, the Mexican nation relies on the good-will of his majesty Napoleon III., Emperor of the French, tc indicate for it another Catholic prince.

"'Given in the Hall of Sessions of the Assembly, on the 10th of July, 1863.

"'TEODOSIO LARES, *President.*

"'ALEJANDRO ARANGO Y ESCANDON, *Secretary.*

"'JOSE MARIA ANDRADE, *Secretary.*'

"Therefore let it be printed, published by national edict, and circulated, and let due fulfilment be given thereto.

"Given at the palace of the supreme executive power in Mexico, on the 11th of July, 1863.

"JUAN N. ALMONTE.
"JOSE MARIANO SALAS.
"JUAN B. ORMAECHEA."

A deputation of the Assembly of Notables immediately proceeded to Europe, sought the Archduke Maximilian, and communicated to him the wishes of the Mexican people. In September, 1863, they thus addressed him:

THE OFFER OF THE MEXICAN CROWN.

Senor Estrada's Address to Maximilian.

"PRINCE:—The powerful hand of a generous monarch had hardly restored liberty to the Mexican nation, when he dispatched us to your imperial highness, cherishing the sincerest wishes and warmest hopes for our mission. We shall not dwell upon the visitations which Mexico has had to undergo, and which, as they are notorious, have reduced our country to the verge of despair and ruin. There are no means we have not employed, no way we have not tried, to escape a situation full of misery for the present, and foreboding catastrophes for the future. We have long endeavored to extricate ourselves from the fatal and ruinous position into which the country had fallen, on adopting, with credulous inexperience, republican institutions, at variance with its natural arrangements, its customs, and traditions; institutions which, though they resulted in the greatness and prosperity of a neighboring nation, have only become a source of trials and desperate disappointments in our case.

"Nearly half a century, Prince, has elapsed, carrying with it for Mexico barren tortures and intolerable humiliation, but without deadening the spark of hope and indomitable vitality in our breasts. Full of unshaken confidence in the Ruler of human destinies, we never ceased to look out for a cure of our ever-growing national malady. We may say we awaited its advent true to ourselves. Our faith was not in vain. The ways of Providence have become manifest, opening up a new era, and exciting the admiration of the greatest minds by an unexpected turn of fortune.

"Once again master of her destinies, Mexico, taught by experience, is at this moment making a last effort to correct her faults. She is changing her institutions, being firmly persuaded that those now selected will be even more salutary than the analogous arrangements which existed at the time she was the colony of a European state. This will be all the more certain if we should be destined to see at our head a Catholic Prince, who, with the high and recognized worth of his character, with the nobility of his feelings, knows how to couple that firmness of will and self-sacrificing devotion which are the inheritance of those only who have been selected by God Almighty, in decisive moments of public danger and social ruin, to save sinking peoples and restore them to a new life. Mexico expects much from the spirit of those institutions which have governed it for three centuries, and which, when they fell, left us a brilliant, but, alas! now spoiled inheritance. The democratic republic endeavored to do away with the traces of former grandeur. But whatever may be our confidence in such institutions, their efficiency will be only perfect when crowned in the person of your imperial highness. A king, the heir of an old monarchy, and representing solid institutions, may render his people happy, even in the absence of distinguished qualities of mind and character; but very different and exceptional qualities are required in a prince who intends to become the founder of a new dynasty and the heir of a republic.

"Without you, Prince — believe it from these lips which have never served the purposes of flattery—without you, all our efforts to save the country will be in vain. Without you will not be realized the generous intentions of a great sovereign, whose sword restored us to liberty and whose powerful arm now supports us in this decisive hour. With you, however, experienced in the difficult art of government, our institutions would become what they ought to be, if the happiness and prosperity of our country are to be guaranteed. With you they would have for their foundation that genuine liberty which is coupled with justice and moderation—not the spurious counterfeit we have become conversant with during half a century's ruinous wars and quarrels. Such institutions, equally as they are in harmony with the spirit of the age, will also become the unshakable corner-stone of our national independence. These sentiments, these hopes, which have been long entertained by all true friends of Mexico, are now in the hearts of all in our country. In Europe, too, whatever sympathies or antipathies may have been roused on the occasion of our present step, there is only one voice in regard to your imperial highness and your noble consort, who, shining by personal worth and high virtues, will share your throne and rule over our hearts. The Mexicans require only to see you in order to love you.

"Faithful interpreters of the longing desire and the wishes of our country, in its name we offer to your imperial highness the crown of Mexico—that crown which a solemn resolution of the Assembly of Notables has of its free will and accord handed over to your imperial highness. Even now that resolution has been confirmed by the assent of many provinces, and will soon be sanctioned by the entire nation. Nor can we forget, Prince, that by a fortunate coincidence of circumstances this great national act is taking place on the day on which Mexico celebrates the anniversary of the victorious appearance of the national army, carrying high the banner of independence and monarchy. May it please your imperial highness to fulfil our prayers and accept our choice. May we be enabled to carry the joyous tidings to a country awaiting them in longing anxiety; joyous tidings not only for us Mexicans, but also for France, whose name is now indissolubly bound up with our history; and gratitude for England and Spain, who began the work of revival; and for the illustrious house of Austria, connected by time-honored and glorious memories with a new continent.

"We do not undervalue the sacrifice to be made by your imperial highness in entering upon so great a task with all its consequences, and in severing yourself from your friends in Europe—that quarter of the globe which, from its centre, diffuses civilization over the world. Yes, Prince, this crown which our love offers you is but a heavy burden to-day, but it will soon be made enviable by your virtues, our zealous co-operation, our loyal devotion, and inextinguishable gratitude. Whatever may be our faults, however deep our fall, we are still the sons of those who, inspired by the sacred names of religion, king, and country, hesitated not to run the greatest risks, engage in the grandest enterprises, combat and suffer in their course. These are the sentiments which, in the name of our grateful country, we lay at the feet of your imperial highness. We offer them to the worthy scion of that powerful dynasty which planted Christianity on our native soil. On that soil, Prince, we hope to see you fulfil a high task, to mature the choicest fruits of culture, which are order and true liberty. The task is great, but greater is our confidence in Providence, which has led us thus far."

Who can read this eloquent address without emotion? It is full of the noblest sentiments of Christian patriotism. The heart of Prince Maximilian was deeply touched by this mark of the attachment of the Mexican people, and he made the following reply:—

Reply of the Archduke Maximilian to the Mexican Deputation.

"*October* 3, 1863.

"Gentlemen:—I am profoundly grateful for the wishes expressed by the Assembly of Notables. It cannot be other than flattering to our house, that the thoughts of your countrymen turn to the descendant of Charles V. It is a proud task to assure the independence and the prosperity of Mexico under the protection of free and lasting institutions. I must, however, recognize the fact—and in this I entirely agree with the Emperor of the French, whose glorious undertaking makes the regeneration of Mexico possible—that the monarchy cannot be re-established in your country on a firm and legitimate basis, unless the whole nation shall confirm by a free manifestation of its will, the wishes of the capital.

"My acceptance of the offered throne must, therefore, depend upon the result of the vote of the whole country. Furthermore, a sentiment of the most sacred of the duties of the sovereign requires, that he should demand for the proposed empire every necessary guarantee to secure it against the dangers which threaten its integrity and its independence. If substantial guarantees for the future can be obtained, and if the universal suffrage of the Mexican people select me as its choice, I shall be ready, with the consent of the illustrious chief of my family, and trusting to the protection of the Almighty, to accept the throne. It is my duty to announce to you now, gentlemen, that in case Providence shall call me to the high mission of civilization which is attached to this crown, it is my fixed intention to open to your country, by means of a constitutional government, a path to a progress based on order and civilization; and, as soon as the empire shall be completely pacified, to seal with my oath the fundamental agreement concluded with the nation.

"It is only in this manner that a truly national policy can be established, in which all parties, forgetting their ancient quarrels, will unite to raise Mexico to the high rank which she should attain under a government whose first principle will be law, based on equity. I beg you to communicate these my intentions, which I have frankly expressed, to your countrymen, and to take measures to obtain from the nation an expression of its will as to the form of government it intends to adopt."

The admirable sentiments of this reply will at once strike the mind of every intelligent person.

Maximilian is not eager to accept the brilliant destiny that is offered to him. He did not seek the Mexican crown, nor does he covet it. He feels the momentous importance of the step which he is invited to take. He does not shrink from the mighty task of creating an empire out of such unpromising materials. He accepts, on two weighty conditions:—1st, on condition that the action of the Assembly of Notables shall be ratified by the whole Mexican people, and 2nd, on condition that the great powers of Europe shall guarantee the stability of the throne that is offered to him.

The reasonableness and justice of these conditions were admitted by the Emperor Napoleon. In his dispatch to General Bazaine, August, 14, 1863, M. Drouyn de Lhuys, the French Secretary of State for Foreign Affairs, says:—"According to the Emperor's ideas, no pressure should be exercised upon the Mexican nation: it alone should have the right of deciding on the form of its institutions, and in case it should adopt a monarchical constitution, on the choice of the prince who should be called to reign over it. We already see, in the vote of the Assembly of Notables, a spontaneous manifestation, and a most imposing one, of its dispositions; but it is important that this vote should be confirmed and ratified as soon as possible by the assent of the people. We likewise applaud the choice of the eminent prince whom the assembly has called to the throne by an acclamation which must, in like manner, receive its definitive approval from the suffrages of the country."

Thus, it will be seen that, before the crown was offered to Maximilian, the Emperor Napoleon had declared that the action of the Assembly of Notables must be confirmed and ratified by the Mexican people: and that the choice of the person also whom they had called to the throne "*must* receive the approval of the suffrages of the country." The same principles are enunciated in still more forcible language, in Napoleon's instructions to General Bazaine, August 17, 1863. He says:—"As I have intimated to you in a previous dispatch, we can consider the action of the Mexican Assembly of Notables, only as the first indication of the disposition of the country. With all the authority which attaches to the eminent men who compose it, the Assembly recommends to its fellow countrymen the adoption of monarchical institutions, and it designates a prince for their suffrages. It belongs to the provisional government to collect those suffrages in such a manner as to banish all doubt in regard to the expression of the will of the country. The best method to be adopted will be that which shall insure the largest manifestation of the popular will in all its independence and sincerity." See Napoleon's instructions to General Bazaine, *ante*, p. 49.

CHAPTER IV.

The Mexican People Vote upon a Change in the Government—Popular Ratification of the Action of the Notables—The Mexican People Pronounce in Favor of Maximilian for Emperor—Manner in which this Election was Conducted—Its Perfect Freedom—Every Mexican Voted—His Election in Mexico Compared with the Elections in Maryland for Three Years past—Two-thirds of the Voters of Maryland Disfranchised—Superior Freedom of the Mexican Election.

THE question was accordingly presented to the Mexican people, and the election took place. The utmost freedom was allowed. Bodies of French troops were present in every Mexican State, but solely in order to keep open the way to the polls. No vote was challenged; no vote was refused. The elections were held at the usual polling places, and the usual local magistrates and judges of election presided. The votes were openly counted, and it was found that the Mexican people had sanctioned the action of the Assembly of Notables, and had, by an almost unanimous vote, pronounced in favor of a monarchy, with Maximilian for Emperor.

Mr. Seward, in a letter to Mr. Dayton, our minister to France, October 23, 1863, thus speaks of this election:—

" M. Drouyn de Lhuys now speaks of an election to be held in Mexico, to result in the choice of Prince Maximilian of Austria to be Emperor of Mexico. We learn from other sources that the prince has declared his willingness to accept an imperial throne in Mexico on three conditions, namely, that he shall be called to it by the universal suffrage of the Mexican nation ; that he shall receive indispensable guarantees for the integrity and independence of the proposed empire: and that the Emperor of Austria shall acquiesce." And Mr. Seward concludes this dispatch with the following significant language, referring to the supposed result of the Mexican election :—"The United States can do no otherwise than leave the destinies of Mexico in the keeping of her own people, and recognize their sovereignty and independence in whatever form they themselves shall choose that this sovereignty and independence shall be manifested."

If this does not mean that the United States will recognize the empire of Mexico if the people choose to have an empire, what does it mean ?

I know it has been said that this Mexican election was held under the glitter of French bayonets. That is true: but, as I have stated, the French bayonets only kept open the way to the polls. The French bayonets did not keep a single Mexican away from the polls. No Mexican was challenged. The vote of no Mexican was refused. It was by far the freest election that had ever taken place in Mexico. Compare it with the elections in Maryland and Missouri from 1863 to 1866.

In Maryland two thirds of the citizens of the State are disfranchised and cannot vote at all.* This is effected by means of a registry law, now in force in that State. This act was passed by the legislature of that State in 1863. The legislature by which it was passed, was elected for the express purpose of passing this registry law. Maryland was not one of the States which seceded. Maryland was not one of the rebel States. Maryland furnished and kept on foot a body of twenty-five thousand troops in the northern army during the whole war. Maryland was represented in Congress during the whole war, by her senators and representatives. Yet from the beginning of the year 1863 to the end of the year 1865, all the elections in Maryland have been controlled by the presence of soldiers, and by military usurpation. During all this time the civil authorities in Maryland exercised no powers except such as it pleased the military authorities to permit them to exercise. The rights of Maryland as a State were entirely taken away. Maryland was changed into a Military Department, and was ruled by a military governor. During the greater part of the period above-named, Maryland was governed by a Mr.

* This was written in 1866.

Schenck, "the hero of Vienna," who, although without military education, military talents, or military experience, had been made a major-general by Mr. Lincoln, and was placed in command at Baltimore, with a large body of troops under his orders. A bitter radical himself, in him the leaders of the radical republican party in Maryland found a ready and willing ally.

There were two parties in Maryland, as there had always been two parties in all the States: the Democratic, or rather the Conservative party, embracing all the old Clay and Webster Whigs; and the Republican, or rather the Radical party, embracing the abolitionists. The latter were in a very small minority. The Conservative, or Democratic party, embraced fully four-fifths of the inhabitants of the State, and all the old residents and persons of property. The Republicans were new settlers, people from the New England States, persons of no property, and comprised, indeed, a class who would have remained forever without influence in the government of the State. Their total strength in 1860 was only two thousand two hundred and ninety-nine votes. In the election for President held in that year, the Democratic candidate for President received ninety thousand two hundred and eight votes, and Lincoln, the Radical candidate, only two thousand two hundred and ninety-nine. That was the last free election that ever took place in Maryland until the election for members of Congress and members of the State Legislature in November, 1866. In 1863, 1864, and 1865, the whole State was overrun by hordes of soldiery from other States, and all the elections were controlled by bayonets.

In 1863, a State constitution was framed by a radical Republican convention, which was utterly repugnant, in its character, to the Democratic citizens of the State. When this constitution was submitted to a vote of the people, it was *rejected* by a majority of one thousand nine hundred and forty-three votes. But there was a body of two thousand five hundred soldiers stationed at and near Baltimore. The military authorities ordered these soldiers to vote, and by their votes a majority of seven hundred and ninety-eight votes was secured *for* the constitution. All of these facts will be found recorded in the newspapers of the day, particularly the New York World, and the Baltimore American, from Oct. 18 to 25, 1863. Thus was a constitution, repugnant to their wishes, and which had actually been rejected by a majority of one thousand nine hundred and forty-three of her own citizens, fastened upon the State of Maryland. The Governor of the State addressed the following letter to the President, on the subject of this military interference with elections in Maryland:—

GOVERNOR BRADFORD TO THE PRESIDENT.

"EXECUTIVE OFFICE, ANNAPOLIS, *Oct.* 31, 1863.

"TO HIS EXCELLENCY, PRESIDENT LINCOLN:—

SIR:—Rumors are to-day current, and they reach me in such a shape that I am bound to believe them, that detachments of soldiers are to be dispatched on Monday next to several of the counties of the State, with a view of being present at their polls on Wednesday next, the day of our State election. These troops are not residents of the State, and consequently are not sent for the purpose of voting; and there is no reason, in my opinion, to apprehend any riotous or violent proceedings at this election; the inference is unavoidable that these military detachments, if sent, are expected to exert some control or influence in that election. I am also informed that orders are to be issued from the Military Department on Monday, presenting certain restrictions or qualifications on the right of suffrage—of what precise character I am not apprised—which the judges of election will be expected to observe. From my knowledge of your sentiments on these subjects, as expressed to Hon. R. Johnson, in my presence, on the 22d instant, as also disclosed in your letter of instructions to General Schofield, since published, in reference to the Missouri election, I cannot but think that the orders above referred to are without your personal knowledge; and I take the liberty of calling the subject to your attention, and invoke your interposition to countermand them. I cannot but feel that to suffer any military interference in the matter of our election, or to prescribe any test of oath to voters, when all the candidates in the State—with the exception, perhaps, of two or three in one Congressional district, are all loyal men—would be justly obnoxious to the public sentiment of the State. There are other reasons why such proceedings would appear as an offensive discrimination against our State. Our citizens are aware that highly important elections have recently taken place in other States, without, it is believed, any such interference by the government authorities, and, if votes by hundreds of thousands have been allowed to be cast there without objection, and with no limit upon the elective franchise, other than the State laws prescribe, and where one, at least, of the candidates so supported was considered so hostile to the government, that for months past he has been banished from the country, certainly any such interference as between the loyal men now candidates in this State, would, under such comparisons, be more justly objectionable, and finds nothing in the present condition of things here to justify it. I rely, therefore, upon your Excellency for such an order as will prevent it. I have the honor to be, with great respect, your Excellency's obedient servant, A. W. BRADFORD.

Governor Bradford also issued the following proclamation:

PROCLAMATION BY GOVERNOR BRADFORD.

"STATE OF MARYLAND, EXECUTIVE DEPARTMENT,
ANNAPOLIS, *Nov.* 2, 1863.

"TO THE CITIZENS OF THE STATE AND MORE ESPECIALLY THE JUDGES OF ELECTION:—

"A military order, issued from the headquarters of the "Middle Department," bearing date the 27th ult., printed and circulated, as it is said, through the State, though never yet published here, and designed to operate on the approaching election, has just been brought to my attention, and is of such a character, and issued under such circumstances as to demand notice at my hands.

"This order, reciting 'that there are many evil disposed persons now at large in the State of Maryland, who have been engaged in rebellion against the lawful government, or have given aid and comfort, or encouragement to others so engaged, or who do not recognize their allegiance to the United States, and who may avail themselves of the indulgence of the authority which tolerates their presence, to embarrass the approaching election, or through it to foist enemies of the United States into power,' proceeds, among other things, to direct 'all provost marshals and other military officers to arrest all such persons found at or hanging about or approaching any poll or place of election on the 4th of November, 1863, and report such arrest to these headquarters.'

"This extraordinary order has not only been issued without any notice to, or consultation with the constituted authorities of the State, but at a time and under circumstances when the condition of the State, and the character of the candidates, are such as to preclude the idea that the result of that election can in any way endanger either the safety of the government or the peace of the community.

"It is a well known fact that, with perhaps one single exception, there is not a Congressional candidate in the State whose loyalty is even of a questionable character, and in not a county of the State outside of the same Congressional district is there, I believe, a candidate for the legislature or any State office whose loyalty is not equally undoubted. In the face of this well known condition of things, the several classes of persons above enumerated are not only to be arrested at, but 'approaching any poll or place of election.' And who is to judge whether voters thus on their way to the place of voting have given 'aid, comfort, or encouragement' to persons engaged in the rebellion, or that they 'do not recognize their allegiance to the United States,' and may avail themselves of their presence at the polls 'to foist enemies of the United States into power?' As I have already said, in a very large majority of the counties of the State there are not to be found among the candidates any such 'enemies of the United States;' but the provost marshals—created for a very different purpose—and the other military officials who are thus ordered to arrest approaching voters, are necessarily made by the order the sole and exclusive judges of those who fall within the prescribed category; an extent of arbitrary discretion, under any circumstance the most odious, and more especially offensive and dangerous in view of the known fact that two, at least, of the five provost marshals of the State are themselves candidates for important offices, and sundry of their deputies for others.

"This military order, therefore, is not only without justification, when looking to the character of the candidates before the people, and rendered still more obnoxious by the means appointed for its execution, but is equally offensive to the sensibilities of the people themselves, and the authorities of the State, looking to the repeated proofs they have furnished of an unalterable devotion to the government. For more than two years past there has never been a time when, if every traitor and every treasonable sympathizer in the State had voted, they could have controlled, whoever might have been their candidates, a single department of the State, or jeopardized the success of the general government. No State in the Union has been or is now actuated by more heartfelt or unwavering loyalty than Maryland—a loyalty intensified and purified by the ordeal through which it has passed; and yet, looking to what has lately transpired elsewhere, and to the terms and character of this military order, one would think that in Maryland, and nowhere else, is the government endangered by the 'many evil disposed persons that are now at large.'

"Within less than a month the most important elections have taken place in two of the largest States of the Union. In each of them candidates were before the people, charged by the particular friends of the government with being hostile to its interests, and whose election was deprecated as fraught with the most dangerous consequences to its success. One of the most prominent of these candidates was considered so dangerously inimical to the triumph of the national cause, that he has been for months past banished from the country, and yet hundreds of thousands of voters were allowed to approach the polls, and to attempt 'to foist such men into power,' and no provost marshals or other military officers were ordered to arrest them on the way, or so far as we have ever heard, even test their allegiance by any oath.

"With these facts before us, it is difficult to believe that the suggestion that the enemies of the United States may be foisted into power at our coming election, was the consideration that prompted this order; but whatever may have been that motive, I feel it to be my duty to solemnly protest against such an intervention with the privileges of the ballot box, and so offensive a discrimination against the rights of a loyal State."

In Governor Bradford's next message to the legislature of Maryland, he thus spoke of these unparalleled outrages:—

"A few days before that election a military order was issued from the army headquarters at Baltimore, which in effect placed the polls under the surveillance and at the command of the military authority.

You will be furnished with a copy of this order, and

it is not necessary further to recite it than to state in general terms that it was to be executed by the military, aided by the provost marshals. They were to arrest voters whom they might consider disloyal in approaching or hanging about the polls; a prescribed form of oath was furnished, without taking which no one, if challenged, could vote; and the several commanding officers were charged to report to headquarters any judge of election who should refuse to administer that oath, or to aid in carrying out that order. The President modified the first part of the order on the Monday preceding the election, but even that modification seemed to receive no attention from those entrusted with its execution, and was in some instances openly disregarded.

"Prominent among the provost marshals to whom the execution of this order was in part committed were several who were themselves candidates for important offices.

"These marshals, appointed for the pupose of the militia enrollment and draft, were placed by the law creating them under the control of the provost marshal general, but to insure the right to employ them about this election order, special authority was obtained from Washington to place them for the time being under the orders of the military authorities.

"I, therefore, on the Monday evening preceding the election, issued a proclamation giving them this assurance, a copy of which is herewith submitted.

"Before the following morning military orders were

sent to the Eastern Shore, directing its circulation to be suppressed, the public papers were forbidden to publish it, and an embargo laid on all the steamers in port trading with that part of the State, lest they might carry it.

"Abuses commenced even before the opening of the polls. On the day preceding the election, the officer in command of the regiment which had been distributed among the counties of the Eastern Shore, and who had himself landed in Kent county, commenced his operations by arresting and sending across the bay some ten or more of the most estimable and distinguished of its citizens, including several of the most steadfast and uncompromising loyalists of the Shore. The jail of the county was entered, the jailer seized, imprisoned, and afterwards sent to Baltimore, and prisoners confined therein under indictment, set at liberty. The commanding officer referred to gave the first clue to the character of disloyalty against which he considered himself as particularly commissioned by printing and publishing a proclamation in which, referring to the election to take place next day, he invited all the truly loyal to avail themselves of that opportunity and establish their loyalty 'by giving a full and ardent support to the whole government ticket upon the platform adopted by the Union League Convention,' declaring that 'none other is recognized by the Federal authorities as loyal or worthy of support of any one who desires the peace and restoration of the Union.'

"To secure the election of that ticket seemed to be

the business to which he and his officers especially devoted themselves throughout the day of election. In the statements and certificates which have been forwarded to me from different counties in that Congressional district, I have been furnished, I presume, with an account of part only of the outrages to which their citizens were subjected. The 'government ticket' above referred to was in several, if not all of these counties, designated by its color; it was a yellow ticket, and armed with that, a voter could safely run the gauntlet of the sabres and carbines that guarded the entrance to the polls, and known sympathizers with the rebellion were, as certified to me, allowed to vote unquestioned, if they would vote that ticket, whilst loyal and respected citizens, ready to take the oath, were turned back by the officers in charge without even allowing them to approach the polls.

"In one district, as appears by certificate from the judge, the military officer took his stand at the polls before they were opened, declaring that none but 'the yellow ticket' should be voted, and excluded all others throughout the day. In another district a similar officer caused every ballot offered to be examined, and unless it was the favored one, the voter was required to take the oath, and not otherwise; and in another again, after one vote only had been given, the polls were closed, the judges all arrested and sent out of the county, and military occupation taken of the town.

"A part of the army which a generous people had supplied for a very different purpose was on that day engaged in stifling the freedom of election in a faithful State, intimidating its sworn officers, violating the constitutional rights of its loyal citizens, and obstructing the usual channels of communication between them and their Executive."

But this was not all. A few months before the election, every Democratic newspaper in the State of Maryland was suppressed by military authority, in contempt of the laws of the State, and in defiance of the constitution of the United States. One only remained, the Evening Post, of Baltimore. This too was suppressed, by the following order:—

"EIGHTH ARMY CORPS, MIDDLE DEPARTMENT.

"BALTIMORE, SEPT. 30, 1864.

"EDITOR EVENING POST:—As the surest means of preventing your office being made the subject of violence, you will discontinue the publication of your paper the Evening Post. By command of

"Major-General WALLACE."

Thus were the Democratic citizens of Maryland deprived of all means of knowing by what conduct on their part the electoral vote of their State might possibly be secured for the Democratic candidates. Mr. Lincoln was a candidate for re-election himself; that part of the army which was stationed in Maryland was under his express orders; and he thus used it, in order to prevent the vote of Maryland from being cast for the Democratic candidates. The editors of the Evening Post immediately came to Washington, to beg the President that he would permit them to resume the publication of the paper. But Mr. Lincoln refused even to see them. Whereupon the Hon. Reverdy Johnson caused the following two letters to be published :—

"BALTIMORE, OCT. 6, 1864.

"*To the President of the United States.*

"SIR :—The accompanying communication from the editor and proprietors of the Evening Post, of this city, has been placed in my hands, with a request to forward it to you. The wrong it discloses seems to me to be so utterly without justification or excuse that I should be doing injustice to you to suppose for a moment that you will permit it to be continued.

"You will also receive with this a copy of the paper issued on the last day on which its publication was permitted, and I am sure you will agree with me in the opinion that it contains nothing of a disloyal character, unless it be that it has at its head the names of Mc Clellan and Pendleton, as its preferred candidates in the present Presidental canvass. It would be my duty to apologize in advance were I even to hint that you would consider that as any evidence of disloyalty, or as affording the slightest grounds for the suppression of the paper.

"The reason assigned for the military order complained of you cannot fail also to agree with me in thinking to be wholly insufficient, since the officer issuing it had under his command two or three thousand armed soldiers, a force abundantly adequate to protect the office of the newspaper and its editor from the violence of a mob, had there been any indication at the time that such violence would be used.

"I am made the organ of bringing this matter to your attention, because of my being one of the Senators of the State, and bound by that relation to do what I can to protect her citizens against outrage.

"An early reply to the request of the editors, sent through me, is respectfully solicited, and, not doubting that it will be a favorable one—I have the honor to remain your obedient servant.

"REVERDY JOHNSON."

NEWSPAPER SUPPRESSION AT BALTIMORE.

"BALTIMORE, OCT. 10, 1864.

"*To the editors of the National Intelligencer:*

"GENTLEMEN:—The papers you receive with this (and which you will do me the favor to publish) speak for themselves, telling a story that no American citizen worthy of the name will read but with deep regret.

"Of the many outrages of like character perpetrated under the authority of the President or with his approval, the suppression of the Evening Post is the most flagrant. The cause assigned (if true) is a sad exhibition of the power of the President to put down a gigantic rebellion having arrayed in its support hundreds of thousands of well disciplined soldiers, commanded by brave and skilful officers. A major-general of the President's appointment, having several thousand soldiers subject to his orders, has not the power, he tells us, to prevent the suppression of a paper by mob violence; and the President, with a want of courtesy not to have been expected, refuses to see the gentlemen whose property and rights as freemen, he was informed, had been outraged, or even to answer respectful letters soliciting his interference.

"Posterity will hardly believe that such things should have occurred, and the people in this country, and everywhere where liberty is valued, will regard it but with shame and indignation. I trust in God that the day is near at hand when the constitution which our fathers bequeathed us, and the freedom which they designed should be perpetual, will be ours once more.

"Yours, with regard,

"REVERDY JOHNSON."

When the election for President took place, the registry law had not yet gone into operation, and the Democratic citizens made every effort to vote. These efforts were frustrated in two cases out of three, over the whole State. The leaders of the radical party in Maryland had sought the aid of the great radical leaders in Congress, and the latter had instructed the military authorities to see to it that no disloyal person was allowed to vote in Maryland. Parties of soldiers were accordingly stationed at every voting place in the State. Whenever a Democrat came up to vote, he was denounced by the radicals present as "disloyal," and was usually hustled away from the polls. About one third of the Democratic voters in the State succeeded in getting their votes in, but fully two thirds were prevented. The judges of the election reported the result of this election as follows: For Lincoln, forty thousand one hundred and fifty-three; for McClellan, the Democratic candidate, thirty thousand seven hundred and thirty-nine. Now it being notorious that there are ninety thousand Democratic voters in the State, it is evident that sixty thousand of them were thus deprived of their votes by the bayonets of a foreign soldiery.

The registry law provides in substance, that no person in Maryland shall be allowed to vote unless his name be registered; and that no person's name shall be registered unless he can give certain prescribed answers to some twenty of the most absurd and ridiculous questions. These questions do not relate to his right to vote at all. They relate to his private opinions, his feelings, his wishes, his hopes, and other nonsense of that kind. Very few Democrats, of course, can answer them to the satisfaction of their political opponents. The law was drawn up by the radical leaders in Maryland for the express purpose of disfranchising the Democratic voters of the State. A State legislature was then elected for the express purpose of passing this law. This election was conducted in the same manner as the one described above. Very few Democrats were allowed to vote; all the radical candidates were elected; and the radical legislature, thus elected, passed the "registry law." While this registry law remains in force, two thirds of the citizens of Maryland are thus deprived of their votes. Compare these elections in Maryland with the election in Mexico, and see which was the freest; which was the most consistent with republican institutions.

The condition of affairs in Maryland, even at as late a day as the 3d of November, 1866, is thus eloquently described by Hon. Reverdy Johnson, in a speech delivered on that day:

"Before the war, every citizen of Maryland possessed the franchise. Now, it is not so. Our people are not all on the same footing, and our present constitution excludes from the franchise a large majority of our citizens. The provisions of the registry law are so stringent that they exclude many who would not be excluded if the constitutional provision on the subject had been fairly carried out. The citizen who, having had a father, son, or brother in the service of the confederates, even felt, during the war, sympathy for his fate, is excluded. He who had entertained the opinion that a State had a right to secede (a doctrine taught by Jefferson, and maintained by many of the best men in every State), is excluded. He who, hearing that a father, son, or brother was suffering from want of food or medicine, and sent him the smallest quantity of either, is excluded. We all remember that most of the registers, with an ignorance or audacity never before exhibited, refused registration upon the most ridiculous pretences. The result was, nearly three fourths of the voters were excluded. In the city of Baltimore, about ten thousand were registered, when its voting population was thirty thousand. And bad as this was, many of those who were registered, at the elections that have since occurred have been denied the right to vote by partisan judges. At the last municipal election, less than eight thousand votes were polled, though the entire voting population was at least forty thousand. Can this condition of things continue? Ought freemen to permit it?"

I am aware that I have made, in this chapter, a long digression. But it is not irrelevant to the subject. It shows, by comparison with the election held in Mexico, in 1863, that the latter was a thousand times more free, and expressed the popular will infinitely more correctly, than the elections held in Maryland for some years past.

CHAPTER V.

Maximilian's Second Condition also Complied with—The Stability of the Mexican Empire Guaranteed by France, Austria, and Belgium—A Deputation of Mexicans Arrive at Miramar—Maximilian Accepts the Mexican Crown—Embarkation of Maximilian for Mexico—The Voyage across the Atlantic—Arrival at Vera Cruz—Reception there—Proclamation of Maximilian on Landing—Arrival at the City of Mexico—Reception there—Rejoicings of the People—Festivities and Illuminations—Immensity of the Task which Maximilian found before him—Measures which he Adopted to Secure the Prosperity and Happiness of the People—Good Effect of these Measures—Revival of Commerce, and of all Branches of Business—Effect of the Encouragement of Industry—Gradual Increase in the Revenues of Mexico.

ON the 10th of April, 1864, Prince Maximilian received the Mexican deputation at Miramar, and formally accepted the crown and throne of Mexico. M. Estrada, president of the deputation, delivered an address, in which he dwelt on the importance of the national vote of Mexico, which had been taken at the request of Maximilian, and which had resulted in the ratification of the action of the Assembly of Notables. Maximilian, replying, said that he felt not the slightest doubt, from the act of adhesion just presented to him, that the immense majority of the country were in favor of the imperial form of government, and of himself as the head of the State. The choice of the country had been laid down, in his reply of October 3d, as one condition of his acceptance; and another was, that full guarantees should be given of his being able to devote himself peaceably to the task of advancing the prosperity of the country. Those guarantees were now fully assured, thanks to the magnanimity of the Emperor of the French, who, during the whole of the negotiations, had shown a straight-forwardness and kindness which he (the speaker) could never forget. "The illustrious head of my family," pursued the archduke, "having given his consent, I now declare that, relying on the assistance of the Almighty, I accept the crown offered me by the Mexican nation. As I stated in my address of October 3d, I shall endeavor to place the monarchy under the authority of the constitutional laws as soon as the pacification of the country shall be complete. The force of a government is, in my opinion, more assured by sound regulations than by the extent of its limits, and I shall be anxious for the exercise of my government to fix such bounds to it as may insure its duration. I shall hold firmly aloft the flag of independence, as the symbol of our future grandeur. I call for the co-operation of all the Mexicans who love their country to aid me in the accomplishment of my noble but most difficult task. Never shall my government forget the gratitude it owes to the illustrious sovereign whose friendly support has rendered the regeneration of our noble land possible. I am now on the point of leaving for my new country, paying, as I go, a visit to Rome, where I shall receive from the holy father that benediction which is so precious for all sovereigns, but above all to me, called, as I am, to found a new empire."

As soon as the archduke had uttered the last word, the deputation and all the Mexicans present acclaimed their new sovereign by crying out three times: "God save the Emperor Maximilian I." "God save the Empress Carlotta!" At the same instant, salutes of artillery, fired from the bastions of the castle, announced to the public the accession of the Archduke Maximilian to the throne of Mexico, and were immediately followed by other salutes from the port and town of Trieste. Then M. Gutierrez de Estrada, as president of the deputation, returned thanks to his majesty for his definitive acceptance of the Mexican crown. He said:

"Sire, this complete and absolute acceptation on the part of your Majesty is the prelude of our happiness; it is the consecration of the salvation of Mexico, of its approaching regeneration, of its future greatness. Every year, on this day, our children will offer up their thanksgivings to heaven in gratitude for our miraculous deliverance. As for us, sire, there remains a last duty to perform, and that is to lay at your feet our love, our gratitude, and the homage of our fidelity."

The arrangements of Maximilian for his voyage across the Atlantic were soon completed, and a few days afterward he embarked, accompanied by the Empress Carlotta, and attended by a brilliant retinue, composed of Mexican, French, and Austrian officers of high rank, many of whom also were accompanied by their wives and daughters. The Emperor of Austria had placed at the service of Maximilian, for this ocean transit, three national vessels, although one of them was of a capacity sufficient to convey the young Emperor, with most of the members of his suite, in perfect comfort. The voyage was a very pleasant one, and was marked by no unusual incidents.

Toward the end of May, 1864, the little fleet reached Vera Cruz in safety, and the distinguished party immediately landed. They were received by the authorities and inhabitants of the city, with every mark of consideration and respect, and Maximilian immediately issued the following proclamation.

"PROCLAMATION.

"MEXICANS:—You have desired my presence. Your noble nation, by a universal vote, has elected me henceforth the guardian of your destinies. I gladly obey your will. Painful as it has been for me to bid farewell forever to my own, my native country, I have done so, being convinced that the Almighty has pointed out to me, through you, the great and noble duty of devoting all my might and heart to the care of a people who, at last, tired of war and disastrous contests, sincerely wish for peace and prosperity—a people who, having gloriously obtained their independence, desire to reap the benefits of civilization and of true progress only to be attained through a stable Constitutional Government. The reliance that you place in me, and I in you, will be crowned by a brilliant triumph if we remain always steadfastly united in courageously defending those great principles which are the only true and lasting basis of modern government, those principles of inviolable and immutable justice, the equality of all men before the law; equal advantages to all in attaining positions of trust and honor, socially and politically; complete and well-defined personal liberty, consisting in protection to the individual and the protection of his property; encouragement to the national wealth, improvements in agriculture, mining, and manufactures; the establishment of new lines of communication for an extensive commerce; and lastly, the free development of intelligence in all that relates to public welfare. The blessing of God, and with it progress and liberty, will not surely be wanting if all parties, under the guidance of a strong National Government, unite together to accomplish what I have just indicated, and if we continue to be animated by that religious sentiment which has made our beautiful country so prominent even in the most troublous periods.

"The civilizing flag of France, raised to such a high

position by her noble Emperor, to whom you owe the new birth of order and peace, represents those principles. Hear what, in sincere and disinterested words, the chief of his army told you a few months since, being the messenger of a new era of happiness: 'Every country which has wished for a great future, has become great and powerful.'

"Following in this course, if we are united, loyal, and firm, God will grant us strength to reach that degree of prosperity which is the object of our ambition.

"Mexicans: The future of your beautiful country is controlled by yourselves. Its future is yours. In all that relates to myself, I offer you a sincere will, a hearty loyalty, and a firm determination to respect the laws and to cause them to be respected by an undeviating and all-efficient authority.

"My strength rests in God and in your loyal confidence. The banner of independence is my symbol; my motto you know already: 'Equal justice to all.' I will be faithful to this trust through all my life. It is my duty conscientiously to wield the sceptre of authority, and with firmness the sword of honor.

"To the Empress is confided the sacred trust of devoting to the country all the noble sentiments of Christian virtue and all the teachings of a tender mother.

"Let us unite to reach the goal of our common desires; let us forget past sorrows; let us lay aside party hatreds, and the bright morning of peace and of well-deserved happiness will dawn gloriously on our new empire.

"MAXIMILIAN.

"VERA CRUZ, *May* 28, 1864."

This proclamation was immediately circulated all over the country, and it had a most happy effect. After being at the mercy of one military adventurer after another, for forty years, whose boundless rapacity had kept them in constant poverty, the Mexican people now hoped that a deliverer had come at last, who would protect them in their persons and property and allow them to pursue the avocations of peace and industry in security. Nor were these bright anticipations disappointed.

On the 12th of June, 1864, the Emperor made his formal entry into the capital of Mexico. Escorted by a brilliant retinue of troops, whose bright uniforms, polished armor, and glittering weapons flashed in the sunlight, and followed by a motley crowd of Indians, dressed in strange and uncouth garments, he rode into the city amid the noise of artillery, and the clashing of musical instruments. After leaving Rio Frio, he and the Empress travelled on horseback for six miles, arriving at the hacienda of Zoquiapan at nightfall, while the rain was falling copiously. On the following day (the 11th) they again left for Ayutla and Guadaloupe, and it was between these two towns that the Indians flocked to join the cavalcade, bearing banners made of palm leaves and calico, and covered with devices and inscriptions in the Mexican language. A number of floral arches were also erected along the road, and on one or two occasions children were sent out with bouquets of fresh flowers to be presented to the Empress, who received them with great kindness and evident satisfaction. Deputations of citizens, male and female, left the city early in the morning to meet the imperial party, and, arriving at Guadaloupe at about noon, added to the activity and brilliancy of the scene.

As soon as the cannon of the fort announced the appearance of the Emperor, the political and municipal authorities went out to greet and welcome him. The archbishops of Mexico and Michoacan and the bishop of Oajaca awaited their majesties at some distance from the door of the church, and on their approach conducted them within its walls under a silken canopy. The church itself was decorated for the occasion in the most complete and expensive fashion, a throne having been erected for the sovereigns. The services of the day began by the intoning of the "Domino salvum fac Imperatorem" by Archbishop Labastida and the other prelates present. At the close of the religious exercises the Emperor returned to the entrance and passed through to the cabildo. Here, in one of the largest saloons, the political prefect of Mexico, Senor Villar de Bocanega, made the following address to the Emperor:

"SIRE:—At the foot of the portentous Cerro of Tepeyac, and divided only by a wall from the temple in which is venerated the protecting mother of the Mexicans, the Guadaloupan virgin, the political prefect of the first department of the empire, the municipal prefect of the great city of Mexico, the ayuntamiento, the archbishop and other authorities, full of the most grateful pleasure, their hearts swelling with joy, present themselves before their beloved sovereigns to welcome them on their happy arrival at the gates of the city in which is erected the throne which the Mexicans have reared for them. Words fail me to express at once our gratitude for abandoning another throne, riches, country, parents, brothers, and friends; and having compassion for our misfortunes, your majesties have deigned to come and try to make us happy, and to save us from the evils which were leading us to disappear from the catalogue of nations. By information and writing your majesties have heard of the will of the people, and now you personally see that you have not been deceived, but that from the shores of Vera Cruz to the gates of the city all acclaim their sovereigns, their enthusiasm having no limits. The Mexicans will continue to do so; and sire, I protest, in the name of the departments under my charge, that we will obey and assist the monarch whom we have chosen."

The Emperor's reply was brief and to the point. He said:

"Profoundly moved by the enthusiastic reception which I have from all the towns and cities in my progress, my emotion and my gratitude acquire new intensity on finding myself at the gates of the capital, to see its principal authorities assembled to congratulate me in a place so respected and so dear to me and the Empress, as it is to all Mexicans. I thank you for your felicitations and salute you with the warmth of one who loves you and who has identified his fate with yours."

At the close of this little speech, which the Emperor spoke with great earnestness, applause burst forth on all sides, accompanied by clapping of hands, and waving of handkerchiefs by the ladies. Such a brilliant sight had seldom been seen in Mexico as the appearance of the city on this occasion. The streets selected for the imperial transit were decorated in the most profuse and dazzling styles of beauty and splendor. Every building, public and private, was closed and hung with flags and banners, mingled with festoons of flowers. The streets and public places were lined with soldiers, French for the most part. Balconies and windows commanding a view of the line of march brought fabulous prices. Churches and church-towers were gaudily decorated, while the bells of the cathedral and other edifices kept up a continual clangor. The palace and public buildings in the square were sumptuously ornamented, and portraits of the Emperor and Empress appeared at many of the windows. To give a full idea of the various decorations of the streets would occupy much more space than is necessary. But it must be confessed that it was a brilliant and successful affair, not only so far as the mere display of taste was concerned, but also because it was accompanied by every manifestation of genuine enthusiasm on the part of a free people.

The arrival of the Emperor was made known by salvos of artillery from in front of the Portales, and as he rode along in an open carriage, with the Empress at his side, the ladies from the balconies and *azoteas* showered down rose-leaves and gold and silver leaves upon them in great profusion. Frequently the streets were so crowded with people that the whole cortege had to stop, and then the Emperor would bow all around to the people in the streets, on the balconies, and on the housetops. Loud cheers and *vivas* resounded in every street through which the brilliant cavalcade passed, and the ladies waved their handkerchiefs and small flags, both French and Mexican. The Emperor rode along the Calle San Francisco to Calle Potrero, and thence direct to the cathedral, where the bishops were prepared to conduct him to the throne there erected for him. The crowds gathered about the square and the palace at this time were very large, but there was no disorder or confusion.

After the celebration of mass, the Emperor received his friends in the national palace, and presented many of them to the Empress. On several distinguished Mexicans he conferred the order of Guadaloupe. General Mejia was among those who were thus honored. Banqueting and festivity filled up the rest of the day, and toward evening the Emperor took a ride in the groves at the end of the city.

The illumination of the capital in the evening was the most brilliant and successful part of the whole demonstration. As darkness fell upon the city, the dwellings on the principal streets were at once transformed into palaces of light and beauty. Brilliancy of color and effect prevailed everywhere. The great square or plaza in front of the palace was decorated and illuminated in excellent style, while the centre of the enclosure was reserved for the display of fireworks to come off at night. The palace itself, as well as the Monte Pio, Portales, Museum, and other public and private edifices in the vicinity, blazed with lights of every order of form, color, and brilliancy. The cathedral, with its old towers flashing out hundreds of lights, was the most attractive of all. From its portals, around its corridors, and to the highest pinnacle of its great belfry, innumerable lamps were suspended, the united effect of so many lights on so great an eminence being very beautiful. The windows of the towers, too, were all thrown wide open, and illuminated; and the bells therein were kept continually revolving and thundering out their loud notes of acclamation.

At eight o'clock, the gathering in the square consisted of many thousands of people. The main street, which traverses the city from the square tó the Alamada, was the scene of much activity, beauty, and attraction. All the houses along its whole length were draped with white and colored curtains, and from the windows, balconies, and *azoteas* floated innumerable national flags, banners, and ensigns. Here and there, at regular distances, gigantic triumphal arches were erected, and, though not all entirely complete or perfect, adorned with a multitude of green boughs, odorous blossoms and fresh flowers, gathered in the extensive gardens around the city. Exquisite bouquets and garlands, skilfully worked in every style of native art, were suspended around the columns, tributes of ingenuity and of loyalty of the Indian peasants, who had gathered the fragrant roses in the bosom of the tranquil mountains. Beneath the gleaming colored light of thousands of lanterns, all these designs and architectural triumphs were seen to great advantage. The principal decorations and illuminations in the Calle de Potrero and the Calle de San Francisco, the one being a continuation of the other, were those of the German Club, the Hotel de Iturbide, and the residences of Messrs. Barron and Escandon, wealthy residents of Mexico. The German decorations were got up with all the taste and elegance for which this people are so famous in all parts of the world. Many of their congratulatory inscriptions were written in the language of "Vaderland," and must, therefore, have been particularly pleasing to the Emperor. M. Escandon's house was ornamented by two splendid oil paintings of Maximilian and Carlotta, very good likenesses indeed, the productions of a Mexican priest. The residence of M. Barron was also artistically illuminated. In the centre were two paintings, more than ten feet high, the one representing Maximilian seated on his throne, attended by figures of Peace and Plenty, and handing to Almonte a scroll of the Constitution. In* the perspective, Napoleon the Third was seen pointing to the valley of Mexico, where a couple of very large oxen were seen ploughing, and a railroad extending in circuitous lines until it was lost in the clouds. The other painting was a representation of the Em-

* See Report on Mexican affairs, in the first volume of "Executive Documents, No. 73," transmitted to Congress, March 20, 1866.

press surrounded by the ladies of the court. The scene along the street, from seven to ten at night, was more like the realization of some fairy dream than of any thing else one could suppose.

Thus was Maximilian welcomed to his capital. From that moment to the present, the attachment of the Mexican people to his person and his government has never wavered, but has, on the other hand, steadily increased. This attachment is based upon the gratitude which the Mexicans feel, for the unwearied zeal with which the Emperor has devoted himself to the advancement of the happiness and prosperity of the people, and upon the success which has attended his endeavors.

The task which Maximilian found before him, on assuming the administration of the government of Mexico, was probably the most difficult that has ever confronted any ruler or chief magistrate of modern times. Everything was in confusion. Forty years of anarchy had destroyed all order and system, in every department of the government. The people were impoverished by the repeated exactions of the republican chiefs who had succeeded each other in the supreme power. Agriculture languished, because to plant, cultivate, and raise a crop, was only to do so for the benefit of some republican guerrilla chief, who would swoop down upon the farmer's barn, and carry off the whole produce of his farm, as soon as it was harvested. The mechanic arts languished, because the incessant civil wars that had prevailed, had compelled nearly all the young men in the country to serve under the banners of one or the other of the contending chiefs, and there were few left at home, either to learn, or to carry on, the useful arts. Commerce languished for the same reason, and, also, because even the most wealthy merchants were liable to be deprived of the fruits of years of labor and enterprise, by the forced loans and forced contributions which were levied incessantly by the republican chiefs; exactions which it was impossible to resist, and for which no redress could be obtained. In a word, every department of industry was paralyzed; the wealth of the country was drained by the chief of whatever republican party happened to be in power, and was lavished to enrich his followers; and no one had any incentive to engage in any of those enterprises which develope the resources, increase the wealth, and add to the prosperity and happiness of other countries.

The Emperor fully comprehended the situation, and set himself resolutely to work to effect a radical change in all these particulars. The principles upon which the government was to be administered, had already been enunciated, and had commended themselves to the approval of every intelligent Mexican. First of all, the Emperor caused it to be distinctly understood, that henceforth every citizen of Mexico was to be protected by the laws, in his person and his property; that life and property were to be secure; and that every one was expected to devote himself with assiduity to his business, without any apprehension of being called upon for compulsory military service. No sooner was this understood, than a marked change took place at once, all over the empire. The merchants, in the large towns, who were fortunate enough to have agricultural implements for sale, were besieged by crowds of farmers anxious to buy ploughs, scythes, forks, shovels, rakes, any thing with which they might resume the cultivation of their long neglected fields. The supply of these articles was soon exhausted; but orders were sent to New York and Philadelphia for fresh supplies, as well as for the more improved descriptions of implements which had not yet been introduced in Mexico. This was the beginning of a trade of this kind, between Mexico and the cities of the United States, which, although, of moderate dimensions during the war, has grown to very large proportions during the last two years. And here is a fact that speaks volumes in favor of the Mexican merchants. Their first purchases were made on credit; necessarily so, for they were so impoverished by their forced "contributions" to the republican chiefs as to be unable to pay in cash; but their bills were always promptly met: and now, and for more than a year past, they both buy and sell for cash. There could not be a stronger proof than this, of the real and substantial benefits which the government of Maximilian has conferred upon the Mexican people.

In every other department of industry in Mexico, the same enterprise began to be exhibited, and with the same encouraging results. The mechanic arts received a powerful impetus. Mexican mechanics have always been noted for their ingenuity, and for the excellence of their workmanship. Encouraged now by the prospect of certain remuneration for their labor, they devoted themselves in all the principal cities and towns, to their respective departments of labor with an assiduity which met with an immediate and generous reward. Before the lapse of many months, hundreds of the Mexican youth, instead of growing up in idleness and crime, were apprenticed by their parents to skilled artisans in the various handicrafts, and are now qualifying themselves for lives of usefulness. The demand for the work of these artisans has steadily increased. Nearly all the furniture used in Mexico is made by them; and they are very skilful workers in gold and silver ware, and in all the various manufactures of iron and brass. The productive industry of this very useful class of citizens is not confined to the capital and the chief cities. In States at a distance from the capital, the same security has been felt, and the same enterprise manifested. During the summer of 1866, and before the Empress Carlotta sailed for Europe, both she and the Emperor were the recipients of many beautiful presents consisting of useful and valuable articles, manufactured by native Mexicans in distant parts of the empire. From Yucatan, the Empress received several handsome workboxes and workstands, made of native Mexican wood, beautifully polished, and inlaid with gold and silver; and a splendid ladies' saddle, which was described to the author, by a gentleman who saw it, as the most superb specimen of saddlery that he had ever seen. A bridle, whip, and elegant saddle-cloth, richly embroidered, all of native Mexican manufacture, accompanied the saddle; and these articles, rich as they were, are only a specimen of the articles that are commonly made by the Mexican artisans.

The commerce of Mexico received at once a powerful impetus. It was to some extent hampered at first, by the existence of the war in the United States. But with the West Indies, with South America, and with several of the European countries, a brisk trade at once sprang up, which has been steadily increasing ever since, and has been, for the last two years, a source of considerable revenue to the imperial treasury.

CHAPTER VI.

Causes of the Success of Maximilian's Government—Severe Measures Adopted against the Guerillas—Good Effect of these Measures—The Authority of the Empire Gradually Extended over the Whole of Mexico —Republican Mexican Soldiers join the Army of Maximilian—Their Reasons for doing so—Construction of Railroads, and Other Works of Internal Improvement—The New Coinage—The Finances—Encouragement Afforded to Education by Maximilian—Encouragement Extended to Literature—Freedom of Religion in Mexico—The Administration of Justice—Publication of the Mexican Laws—Admirable Features of the Mexican Code—The Empress Carlotta—Her Visit to Yucatan.

THE success which has attended the administration of the government of Mexico during the last three years, may be attributed to two causes: first to the indomitable energy and perseverance of the Emperor Maximilian himself and to his admirable and unusual administrative qualities; and to the incomparably noble manner in which all his efforts have been seconded by his devoted and affectionate wife, the Empress Carlotta:—and second, to the fact that he has been fortunate in having around him a body of Mexican gentlemen, both in and out of his cabinet, who are truly and honestly devoted to the interests of their country; and who, with unselfish patriotism, have consecrated their lives to its service. Every monarch, no matter how active he may be, must, to some extent, see with the eyes, and hear with the ears of other people. Maximilian has travelled considerably in Mexico, and has seen and heard for himself, as much as possible, of the condition of the country and the people: but he has derived immense advantage from the information and suggestions furnished to him by the Mexican gentlemen to whom I have alluded, who, of course, are perfectly acquainted with all that relates to the interests of the country.

In the organization of his government, Maximilian wisely availed himself of the services of these Mexican gentlemen, as well as of the experienced statesmen and financiers who had been sent to his assistance by the Emperor Napoleon. His council of Ministers, and his council of State, were thus composed of the very men who were best qualified to give proper direction to the various measures necessary to carry on the government.

There were three subjects, which seemed to demand the immediate attention of the Emperor. These were the finances, military operations, and the treatment of the robbers and guerrillas by whom the roads in Mexico were infested.

A year had elapsed since the capture of Mexico by General Forey, and the defeat and dispersion of the republican army. During that time the French forces in Mexico had been actively engaged in pursuing the remnants of the republican troops, who, broken up into small detachments, roamed all over the country, robbing and murdering travellers, and plundering and burning houses, and even villages. This kind of warfare, on the part of the French troops, was exceedingly laborious and unprofitable, and was attended by few decisive results. The guerrillas, by their superior knowledge of the roads and mountain passes, almost uniformly escaped capture. They always retreated before the French, and thus drew them on, many a weary mile, through difficult mountain passes, and then at last eluded them.

The atrocities which they committed were horrible. Robbery and murder were the least of their crimes. The outrages which they committed on the helpless women who fell into their hands, were too dreadful to speak of in detail; but these atrocities roused against them the anger of every Mexican. The Emperor therefore issued the following proclamation and decree, on the 2d and 3d of October, 1865.

"PROCLAMATION OF HIS MAJESTY THE EMPEROR.

"MEXICANS:—The cause which Don Benito Juarez defended with so much valor and constancy has already succumbed under the force, not only of the national will, but also of the very law which that officer invoked in support of his pretensions. To-day even the faction into which the said cause degenerated is abandoned by the departure of its chief from the native soil.

"The national government for a long time was lenient and exercised great clemency, in order to give the chance to misled and misinformed men to rally to the majority of the nation and to place themselves anew in the path of duty. It has fulfilled its object; the honorable men have assembled under its banner, and have accepted the just and liberal principles which regulate its politics. The disorder is only maintained by some leaders carried away by unpatriotic passions, and assisted by demoralized persons who cannot reach to the level of political principles, and by an unprincipled soldiery, the last and sad remnants of the civil wars.

"Hereafter the contest will only be between the honorable men of the nation and the gangs of criminals and robbers. Clemency will cease now, for it would only profit the mob who burn villages, rob and murder peaceful citizens, poor old men and defenceless women.

"The government, resting on its power, from this day will be inflexible in its punishments, since the laws of civilization, the rights of humanity, and the exigencies of morality demand it.

"MEXICO, *October* 2, 1865. MAXIMILIAN."

"MAXIMILIAN, EMPEROR OF MEXICO.

"HAVING heard our council of ministers and our council of state, we decree.

"ARTICLE 1. All persons belonging to armed bands

or corps, not legally authorized, whether they proclaim or not any political principles, and whatever be the number of those who compose the said bands, their organization, character, and denomination, shall be tried militarily by the courts-martial; and if found guilty even of the only fact of belonging to the band, they shall be condemned to capital punishment within the twenty-four hours following the sentence.

ART. 2. Those who, belonging to the bands mentioned in the previous article, will be captured with arms in their hands, shall be tried by the officer of the force which has captured them, and he shall, within a delay never extending over twenty-four hours after the said capture, make a verbal inquest of the offence, hearing the defence of the prisoner. Of this inquest he will draw an act, closing with the sentence, which must be to capital punishment, if the accused is found guilty, even if only of the fact of belonging to the band. The officer shall have the sentence executed within the twenty-four hours aforesaid, seeing that the criminal receive spiritual assistance. The sentence having been executed, the officer shall forward the act of inquest to the minister of war.

"Art 3. From the penalty established in the preceding articles shall only be exempted those who, having done nothing more than being with the band, will prove that they were made to join it by force, or did not belong to it, but were found accidentally in it.

"ART. 4. If, from the inquest mentioned in article two, facts are elicited which induce the officer holding it to believe that the prisoner was made to join the band by force, without having committed any other crime, or that he was found accidentally in it, without belonging to it, the said officer shall abstain from passing sentence, and he shall send the accused, with the respective act of inquest to the proper court-martial in order that the trial be proceeded with by the latter, in conformity with article one.

"ART. 5. Shall be tried and sentenced conformably with article one of this law: 1st. All those who will voluntarily assist the *guerrilleros* with money, or any other means whatever. 2d. Those who will give them advice, information, or counsel. 3d. Those who voluntarily, and knowing that they are *guerrilleros*, will put within their reach, or sell them arms, horses, ammunition, subsistence, or any articles of war whatever.

"ART. 6. Shall also be tried conformably with the said article 1st: 1. Those who will hold with the *guerrilleros* such relations as infer connivance with them. 2. Those who voluntarily and knowingly will conceal them in their houses or estates. 3. Those who, by word, or writing, will spread false or alarming reports, by which public order may be disturbed, or will make against it any kind of demonstration whatever. 4. All owners or administrators of rural estates who will not give prompt notice to the nearest authority of the passage of some band through the same estates. Those included in paragraphs 1st and 2d of this article shall be punished by imprisonment from six months to two years, or by hard labor from one to three years, according to the gravity of the case. Those who, being included in paragraph 2d, were the ascendants, descendants, spouses, or brothers of the party concealed by them, shall not suffer the penalty aforesaid, but they shall remain subject to the vigilance of the authorities during the time the court-martial will fix. Those included in paragraph 3d of this article shall be punished by a fine of from twenty-five to one thousand dollars, or by imprisonment from one month to one year, according to the gravity of the offence. Those included in paragraph 4th of this article shall be punished by a fine of from two hundred to two thousand dollars.

"Art 7. The local authorities of the villages who will not give notice to their immediate superiors of the passage through their villages of armed men will be ministerially punished by the said superiors by a fine of from two hundred dollars to two thousand dollars, or by seclusion from three months to two years.

"Art. 8. Whatever resident of a village who, having information of the proximity or passage of armed men by the village, will not give notice of it to the authorities, shall suffer a fine of from five to five hundred dollars.

"Art. 9. All residents of a village threatened by some gang, who are between the ages of eighteen and fifty-five years, and have no physical disability, are obliged to present themselves for the common defence as soon as called, and for failing to do so they shall be punished by a fine of from five to two hundred dollars, or by imprisonment of fifteen days to four months. If the authorities think it more proper to punish the village for not having defended itself, they may impose upon it a fine of from two hundred to two thousand dollars, and the said fine shall be paid by all those together, who, being in the category prescribed by this article, did not present themselves for the common defence.

"Art. 10. All owners or administrators of rural estates, who, being able to defend themselves, will not prevent the entrance in the said estates, of *guerrilleros* or other malefactors; or, after these have entered, will not give the immediate information of it to the nearest military authority; or it will receive on the estates the tired or wounded horses of the gangs, without notifying the said authority of the fact, shall be punished for it by a fine of from one hundred dollars to two thousand dollars, according to the importance of the case; and if it is of great gravity, they shall be put in prison and sent to the court-martial, to be tried by the latter conformably with the law. The fine shall be paid to the principal administrator of rents to which the estate belongs. The provision of the first part of this article is applicable to the populations.

"Art. 11. Whatever authorities, whether political, military, or municipal, shall abstain from proceeding, in conformity with the provisions of this law, against parties suspected or known to have committed the offences provided for in said law, will be ministerially punished by a fine of from fifty dollars to one thousand dollars; and if it appear that the fault was of such a nature as to import complicity with the criminal, the said authorities will be submitted, by order of the government, to the court-martial, to be tried by the latter, and punished according to the gravity of the offence.

"Art. 12. Thieves shall be tried and sentenced in conformity with article 1st of this law, whatever may be the nature and circumstances of the theft.

Art. 13. The sentence of death pronounced for offences provided for by this law shall be executed within the delays prescribed in it, and it is prohibited that any demands for pardon be gone through. If the sentence is not of death, and the criminal is a foreigner even after its execution, the government may use toward him the faculty it has to expel from the territory of the nation all obnoxious strangers.

"Art. 14. Amnesty is granted to all those who may have belonged, and may still belong, to armed bands, if they present themselves to the authorities before the 15th of November next, provided they have not committed any other offences subsequently to the date of the present law. The authorities will receive the arms of those who will present themselves to accept the amnesty.

"Art. 15. The government reserves the faculty to declare when the provisions of this law will cease.

"Each one of our ministers is charged with the execution of this law in the part which concerns him, and will give the necessary orders for its strict observance.

"Given at the palace of Mexico on the 3d of October 1865. "MAXIMILIAN."

The good effects of the course thus determined upon were immediately apparent. During the course of the ensuing six weeks, several hundred men, who belonged to these guerrilla bands, voluntarily came in, gave up their arms, received the executive clemency, and began to engage once more in the pursuits of honest industry. It was a remarkable circumstance that almost all those who thus eagerly embraced the opportunity of withdrawing from a life of crime, were young men, mostly from twenty to twenty-five years of age They stated that they had been forced to enter the republican army, and on the defeat and dispersion of that army had been persuaded by their older comrades to join the guerilla bands. So far as is known, all of them have become honest and useful citizens.

The remnants of the guerilla bands now withdrew themselves to the more remote parts of the empire, and the principal roads were no longer infested by their presence. The operations against them were continued with great vigor, and whenever any of them were captured they were summarily dealt with.

The military operations were conducted under the direction of General Bazaine. Although the main army of the republic had been destroyed and its fragments dispersed, there yet remained in the field, in various parts of the empire, certain detachments of republican troops, who continued to be a source of considerable trouble. Juarez himself, with a few hundred men, had retreated from Mexico to San Luis Potosi; from San Luis to Zacatecas; from Zacatecas to Saltillo; from Saltillo to Monterey; from Monterey to Chihuahua. This place was at such a distance from the City of Mexico (nine hundred miles by the roads, or as far as from New Orleans to Chicago), that it was a work of the greatest difficulty to carry on military operations over so great an extent of country; and therefore Juarez was able to remain at Chihuahua for several months. During the summer of 1865, however, he was driven from that place by a few regiments of French troops, and escaped to El Paso del Norte, on the extreme northern frontier of Mexico. By the month of September, 1865, he was compelled to leave that place also, and, crossing the Rio Grande, he fled for some distance into Texas. It was then that the Emperor Maximilian issued the proclamation of October 2d, quoted above.

By that time, the good effects of Maximilian's mild but firm government had begun to be felt in all parts of the empire The Mexican people of all classes saw, that, for the first time in forty years, Mexico had a good government, a government which had at heart the happiness and prosperity of the people. Thousands of the Mexican citizens who had heretofore been attached to the republic, now gave in their adhesion to the empire; and besides this, hundreds of soldiers deserted the various detachments of republican troops that still maintained their organization, and asked to be allowed to take service under Maximilian. A gentleman who has lived many years in Mexico, has related to the author a conversation which he had with one of these deserters, who, at that time, was a sergeant in one of Maximilian's Mexican regiments. He found the man very intelligent, and when he asked him why he had wished to join Maximilian's army, he replied, "Because I and my comrades had learned what the Emperor had done for Mexico; how the country was prosperous and happy wherever his authority extended, and how the Empress was exerting herself to build up and support schools and factories." The feelings of this humble Mexican soldier were no doubt the feelings of thousands of his comrades and countrymen. A letter from Mexico, written at this time, says:

"The work of pacification is progressing satisfactorily in several departments of the empire. The States of Oajaca, of Colima, and of Sonoro are now, after years of bloody conflicts, enjoying a certain degree of peace and security. Guerillas have disappeared from most of the districts, and the population is pursuing with great energy the few bands who remain yet in the mountains.

"The imperialists are in hope to crush the guerillas in the opening campaign, and in less than a year succeed in completely pacifying the country. They base their confidence upon the fact that a year ago Juarez was still in possession of several States and cities from which he has been expelled without trouble or resistance, most part of the time by the inhabitants themselves, and without the assistance of the French. They say that, during these twelve months, the cities of Matamoras, Monterey, and Mazatlan have been occupied, the State of Talisco completely pacified, the State of Oajaca conquered, Sonoro submitted, and the last organized corps of the Juarists destroyed or dispersed. Juarez himself, compelled to leave the central part of Mexico, has so little expectation of causing any portion of the people, however small, to rise in his behalf, that he deems it prudent to run to the frontier and to place himself under protection of the guns placed along the Texan shore."

Such a thing as a railroad in Mexico was unknown before the advent of Maximilian. But at a very early period of his administration he devoted his attention to this subject. By offering encouragement to capitalists and engineers, he soon had several lines of railway undertaken, on all of which satisfactory progress has been made. The principal line is the one from Vera Cruz to the capital. Of this, one half of the distance is now completed and in operation. This road is being built by the eminent engineers, Smith, Knight & Co., of London. The solid and substantial character of the work may be inferred from the fact that one of the bridges, near Orizaba, constructed entirely of iron, is nine hundred feet long and three hundred feet high.

Other works of internal improvement were at once commenced, and carried on with vigor under the direction of the government. The roads and canals were repaired and improved; an improved system of drainage was adopted for the capital, and the city of Mexico was adorned and beautified by the establishment of a new and extensive park, which owes its existence to the liberality and public spirit of the Empress.

The finances were placed in charge of M. Langlais, a very able French financier, who speedily brought order out of confusion. Under his wise and judicious administration, the revenues of the country were placed upon such a basis as very soon afforded a satisfactory income. M. Langlais unfortunately died some months ago; but before his death he had the satisfaction of reporting to the Emperor that the revenue of Mexico was now ample to support the government and leave a surplus for the payment of the foreign liabilities.

Mexico does not enjoy the blessing of "greenbacks," or national bank-notes thirty-seven cents below par; nor do the Mexicans have the luxury of a fractional currency. They are obliged to content themselves with the old-fashioned gold and silver coins as a circulating medium. Maximilian has kept the mints busy ever since his accession; and in the spring of 1866 he began to coin the new gold and silver pieces that are now in circulation. The new silver dollar, and the twenty dollar gold coin, are both beautiful specimens of coinage, bearing on one side the head of the Emperor, and on the other the time-honored Mexican sentiment, "God and Liberty."

During the first journeys which the Emperor and Empress took, in various parts of Mexico, they were impressed with the fact that the cause of education throughout the country needed great encouragement. That encouragement they have afforded in the most liberal and munificent manner. Schools and academies have been everywhere established, even in such remote States as Yucatan, and liberal provision has been made for their support; and all the colleges in Mexico have received large endowments from the imperial purse. A letter from Mexico, in April, 1866, says:

"LIBERALITY OF THE EMPEROR AND EMPRESS.

"Their majesties expended a large portion of their yearly salary—five hundred thousand dollars—in works of charity, donations to schools and benevolent institutions, and works of public improvement. The Alameda of this city, one year since, was a disgrace to any country village, being nothing more than a few dilapidated fountains in an ugly, gnarled wood, destitute of a single ornament or walk that was safe for a foot passenger The Empress determined to remedy this, and ordered the grounds to be put in complete order, paying the expenses out of her private purse. The fountains have been repaired, the pavements relaid, trees pruned and trimmed, and the entire ground decorated with plants, flowers, and trees, until a more lovely silvan spot can scarce be imagined. Thousands of citizens resort here every morning for health or recreation, and what was a few months since carefully avoided has become the fashionable promenade and morning drive for all classes of Mexicans. The Plaza which, three months since, was merely a bare paved square, destitute of ornament, is fast assuming a new aspect. The whole pavement has been taken up, new walks laid, the spaces between the walks filled with trees, flowers, and shrubbery, fountains erected, and in the centre is to be placed a group of statuary, representing the leading spirits of the Mexican revolution—all the design and work of Mexican artists."

In order to afford encouragement and give an impulse to dramatic art, the Emperor has commenced the erection of a superb theatre, and has offered two prizes, of two thousand dollars each, for the best tragedy and comedy. He is truly a man of noble impulses, and has the good of his people at heart. His ambition is to make Mexico a power upon the Western continent second only to the United States, and to leave behind him the name of a human benefactor.

The Catholic religion is the religion of the State, but all religions are tolerated. Every one in Mexico can freely worship God according to the dictates of his own conscience. The Episcopalian, the Presbyterian, and the Methodist is equally protected in the enjoyment of his religion with the Catholic; and the ministers there are not required to take "test oaths" before they can preach the gospel.

The administration of justice throughout the empire is provided for by the Emperor with peculiar care. The judges of the courts are required to be men learned in the law, experienced in the management of causes, and of unblemished integrity. Whereever the authority of the empire extends, justice between man and man is speedily administered, and no man's cause is delayed. Such a state of things has heretofore been unknown in Mexico, under any republican government.

Every encouragement has been afforded by the Emperor to the great work of the codification and systematic arrangement of the Mexican laws. This work has been accomplished by a board of the most learned Mexican lawyers, and is now complete. The entire code forms a body of ten large octavo volumes, which have recently been printed, published, and bound, in the city of Mexico. The paper, typography, and binding of these volumes are in the first style of art, and would do credit to any publishing house in New York or Philadelphia. This code of laws embraces first, all the Mexican laws of a public and general nature, which were in force at the time when the present government was established; and second, those that have been subsequently enacted by the authority of the imperial government. The whole body of laws is said to be based upon the plan of the Code Napoleon, and to possess many of the merits of that incomparable work.

There is a deep significance in the emission of these handsome volumes. They represent the energy and intellect which Maximilian has infused into the administration of the laws of Mexico. These decrees and laws, particularly those enacted during the last two years, are replete with the wise forethought and intelligent progress of the empire. And they are not merely laws on paper. They have been put in execution, and their good effects have been felt in every department of the government, and reach to every Mexican State. Everything, it would seem, has been remodelled by these laws, and placed upon a better basis. Whoever would know the spirit and stamina of the imperial government, should consult these volumes. Their contents embrace every subject, and reveal the industry, the tact, and the remarkable ability of their author; for the Emperor Maximilian is the originator of nearly every one of the recent laws. Here may be found the organic law of the empire, to the strict observance of which Maximilian has pledged himself.*

While upon the subject of book publications, it may be stated that this is a branch of business that has grown up entirely during the last three years. There are two houses in the city of Mexico that have found encouragement enough to warrant them in publishing school-books and literary works to a considerable extent. Among their recent publications are the complete works of the celebrated Spanish author, Gonzales; among them, "El Pastero de Madriga," and "Lucrezia Borgia." Also an excellent translation, in Spanish, by a Mexican gentleman, of Victor Hugo's "Travailleurs de la Mer," under the title of "Los Trabajadores de la Mar," which is a little nearer the original than "Toilers of the Sea."

Allusion has heretofore been made to the very great assistance which Maximilian has derived from the devoted and zealous co-operation of his wife, the Empress Carlotta. This admirable lady, tenderly nurtured, and accustomed all her life to the perfumed air of courts and the luxuries of royalty, devoted herself at once, with all the energy of her nature, to the great work in which her honored husband was engaged. She accompanied him everywhere; saw with her own eyes the wants of the people; alleviated suffering and distress

---

* Letter to "New York News."

wherever she encountered it; encouraged industry by her smiles; stimulated the children and youth to assiduity in their studies by her frequent presence in the school-houses; and quickened the genius of Mexican artists and men of letters, by her munificent rewards for their works.

In November, 1865, she undertook a journey to the distant State of Yucatan, that the people there might see that their welfare was not overlooked by the Emperor. Everywhere she was received with the most enthusiastic expressions of the love and devotion of the people.

While at Merida her majesty donated the following sums: two thousand five hundred dollars for the establishment of a free school for girls in that city; three thousand dollars to the general hospital; three thousand dollars to be distributed among the poor, in especial to such as had suffered by the war of castes; one thousand dollars toward completing the work on the cathedral, and smaller sums to various religious orders.

On the 1st of December, the Empress visited the Agricultural and Industrial Exhibition, and the following day she was present at the benediction and inauguration of the "Constancia" cotton spinning establishment.

Her majesty left Merida on the morning of December 4th, for the city of Campeche, passing through

Uxmal. A large number of the young men of Merida volunteered to attend the Empress as far as the limits of the department as a guard of honor.

A letter from Merida, the capital of Yucatan, thus describes the reception of the Empress at that ancient city:

"Her majesty was elegantly but simply attired, wearing a white dress trimmed with light blue, her noble head being covered with a graceful little hat, also set off with blue. Not a gem or jewel was to be seen upon her graceful person. At the back of her head, beneath the little hat, her well combed auburn hair was noticeable.

"After receiving the congratulations of the delegations mentioned, her majesty advanced into the city, in the midst of the liveliest acclamations, the cortege being swelled by various deputations and by a large number of distinguished persons following in sumptuous carriages of various colors.

"It would take much space to describe the order of the carriages in the procession, the innumerable shouts of welcome resounding in the air, and the cordial greetings uttered by the dense multitude, right and left, during the passing of the imperial cortege at a foot pace from the first triumphal arch to the Plaza de Jesus.

"There her majesty alighted from her carriage, and was received by another delegation of ladies and an angelic bevy of little children.

"While passing by the Government Palace a shower of natural and artificial flowers, of ribbons, bearing appropriate mottoes, and of strips of paper printed with verses, almost inundated our august Empress.

"From the base of the arch to the main entrance to the cathedral her majesty passed between a double line formed by the chief local authorities, presided over by the Political Prefect, Senor Don Jose Garcia Morales.

"His Excellency Don Jose Salazar Harrequi, the Imperial Commissioner, and General Severo del Castillo, commanding the Seventh provincial division, accompanied her majesty, together with the other persons of the court in her suite.

"The military were dressed in full uniform.

"At about eleven o'clock her majesty was received upon the steps of the porch of the temple by the apostolic administrator of the diocese, Dr. Leandro Rodriguez de la Salu, the venerable ecclesiastical chapter, and all the clergy of the capital, in their splendid vestments, preceded by the Cross and a number of wax tapers.

"Kneeling upon a crimson velvet cushion bordered with gold fringe and placed upon a rich carpet, her majesty kissed the holy crucifix presented to her and entered the edifice under a canopy, the poles supporting which were borne by the judges of the Superior Court and the members of the government council of the district. Upon entering the precincts of the temple her majesty devoutly received the holy water offered her.

"In the chancel a rich canopy was prepared, and after the prayers customary upon the reception of sovereigns and a chant accompanied by the solemn music of the organ, worship was offered to Him through whose will all sovereigns reign, during which the Empress remained kneeling in a most devout attitude.

"Thereafter a solemn *Te Deum*, expressly composed for the occasion, was performed.

"The vast cathedral was filled with a numerous assemblage, comprising persons belonging to the highest as well as the lowest degrees of society, collected together to bless and welcome our august sovereign.

"Upon the conclusion of the religious ceremonies her majesty proceeded on foot (dismissing the carriage which awaited her at the foot of the steps) to the residence placed at her disposal—one of the most elegant and capacious mansions in the city.

"Shortly after noon her majesty reached her quarters, where she was greeted with another shower of flowers, ribbons and verses, accompanied by the exquisite music of a military band and the joyful shouts of thousands of both sexes.

"A just tribute to her merit, virtue, beauty and goodness of heart.

"Shortly afterward her majesty received the congratulations of the officials of the district, in an apartment specially arranged for the purpose, after which a large number of ladies, military and civil officers and citizens paid their respects to the Empress.

"In reply to the congratulatory address delivered by the Political Prefect, her majesty, after appearing on the balcony of her apartments at the clamorous request of the multitude without, expressed herself as follows :—

"'We have long wished to visit you in order to study your necessities and learn your desires. The Emperor being prevented from effecting this important object, has sent me to you to present to you his cordial greetings.

"'I assure you from my heart that he deeply regrets that he cannot be here with me, to tell you how great is his affection toward you. He will regret it still more when I inform him of the enthusiastic reception you have given me. He desires, and by all means will endeavor to secure, the prosperity and happiness of the people of Yucatan.'"

We shall soon see the Empress discharging a mission, of still greater importance, for the welfare of Mexico.

CHAPTER VII.

Arms and Ammunition Shipped to the Mexican Liberals from New York —The Steamer Everman—Attempts of the Radicals in Congress to Loan Thirty Millions of Government Funds to Juarez—Measures Taken by Maximilian to Supply the Place of the French Troops—The Emperor Anticipates Intervention by the United States in Favor of Juarez—Mission of the Empress Carlotta to Europe—Sickness of the Empress—Embarrassing Situation of Affairs in Mexico—Outrages of the Mexican Liberals—Sickness of the Emperor—He Retires to Orizaba—The Sherman and Campbell Mission to Mexico—Mr. Campbell's Instructions—Utter Failure of the Mission—Results of the Mission—It Demonstrated the Attachment of the Mexican People to Maximilian—The Question of Abdication Presented to Maximilian—He Refuses to Abdicate—Generous Conduct of the Clergy and Merchants—Encouraging Prospects of the Empire.

THE objection that is most easily and most frequently raised against the government of Maximilian, is, that it has not yet succeeded in conquering the prejudices of all the Mexicans, and that the republicans in Mexico still keep troops in the field, and even gain some victories over the imperial troops. This is true, to some extent; and the explanation of the fact is by no means creditable to the United States. These "liberal successes" have all taken place during the last few months, and are the result of direct interference in behalf of Juarez on the part of citizens of the United States. Armed expeditions were fitted out in New York, and cargo after cargo of arms and ammunition was sent to Mexico. It is believed that one of these expeditions was under the command of a major-general late of the United States army, whose gallant and intrepid conduct, and admirable dispositions at Monocacy, saved Washington from capture by the Confederates, and who is now understood to be following the fortunes of Juarez.

But it is not material aid, alone, that the Juarists have derived from the United States. During the first session of the thirty-ninth Congress, beginning in December, 1865, persistent and strenuous efforts were made by Mr. Thaddeus Stevens, Mr. Schenck, and other leading radical republicans, to induce Congress to appropriate thirty millions of dollars for the cause of the Mexican republic—or, in other words, to authorize the government to endorse certain Juarist bonds to that amount. These bonds were utterly worthless, and the endorser, of course, would be called upon to pay them. The scheme never received the approval of Congress. But its agitation, both in Congress and in the newspapers of the north, served the purpose for which the friends of the Juarists had introduced it. Juarez himself, and his followers in Mexico, are thus encouraged to hope that the United States government will, at some period not very distant, intervene in their behalf, and by actual armed interposition, as well as by the advances of large sums of money, assist them in overthrowing the present government of Mexico, and in re-establishing the republic. These hopes have been greatly cherished and strengthened, 1st, by the extraordinary conduct of General Sheridan on the Rio Grande, in the interests of Juarez: and 2d, by the recent mission of General Sherman and Mr. Campbell to Vera Cruz. Stimulated by the hopes thus afforded, Juarez and his officers have succeeded in keeping in the field a force of a few thousand men, with whom the recent "liberal successes" have been achieved. These men are the most reckless and desperate characters that can be found in Mexico; robbers, thieves, murderers and assassins. Almost every paper that comes from Mexico, is filled with the records of their atrocities. They are allowed the utmost license to plunder the inhabitants, and whenever they capture a town or village, it is given up to their unlicensed rapacity. The outrages which they thus committed at Hermosillo, a few months since, are already fresh in the public mind. Such are the "soldiers of the republic," in behalf of whom the sympathies of the American people are invoked.

In the early part of the year 1866, the Emperor Maximilian was made aware of the determination of the French government to withdraw the French troops from Mexico during the course of the year

1867. This event, however, had been anticipated by Maximilian, and already measures were in progress by which the Emperor hoped to supply the places of the French troops by an army which should be essentially Mexican—a national Mexican army. The arrangements for the organization of this army proceeded during the whole of the year 1866. By the end of that year there were organized into regiments twenty-six thousand native Mexicans, all good soldiers, well disciplined, and acquainted with military life and duties. These were divided into four divisions, and each division placed under the command of a competent general. The principal officers of the regiments were for the most part Frenchmen and Austrians; but in the grade of captains and lieutenants there were many Mexican gentlemen. Although the French army, as an organization, was to be withdrawn, yet the Emperor Napoleon had given permission to all the officers and men who chose to do so, to volunteer and enter the Mexican army, and up to the end of the year 1866, about eight thousand men had signified their intention to do so: so that Maximilian counted upon having an effective army of thirty-five thousand men, ready to take the field by the spring of 1867, if the French troops should be withdrawn as soon as that.

It became a very serious question, however, whether the Mexican government could maintain itself, after the departure of the French army. There was no doubt of the efficiency of the newly organized Mexican army; there was no doubt of the attachment of the great body of the Mexican people to Maximilian and his government. If left alone, without interference from abroad, there was no doubt that the government could maintain itself without serious difficulty. But there was too much reason to fear that interference on the part of the United States was to be expected, as soon as the French troops should have left Mexico. The Emperor Napoleon had, indeed, before he had made the final arrangements for the withdrawal of the French troops from Mexico, inquired of the United States government whether, in case of such withdrawal, neutrality on the part of the latter, toward Mexico, would be observed: and Mr. Seward, Secretary of State, had replied in plain words, that, in case the French troops should be withdrawn from Mexico, the United States would observe absolute neutrality toward that country, and would allow the Mexican people to settle for themselves, the form of their government. But the Emperor Maximilian placed very little reliance upon this promise; and he anticipated that active interference on the part of the United States, in favor of the Juarist faction, might be expected the moment after the French army should have embarked. The event showed that these anticipations were well founded.

There were other weighty questions connected with

the future stability of the empire, that gave Maximilian much concern; and it was finally agreed, in the summer of 1866, that the Empress Carlotta should herself proceed to Europe, in order that, by personal interviews with the Emperor of France and the Emperor of Austria, these questions might be placed upon a basis of satisfactory settlement. This journey was accordingly undertaken. The Empress embarked on board the French mail steamer "Empress Eugenia," on the 13th of July, and in due time reached Paris. In the course of three months, the main objects of her mission to Europe had been successfully accomplished. Her last letter to the Emperor Maximilian stated in substance, that although every thing they had hoped for had not been gained, yet that the results that she had accomplished were quite sufficient to compensate her for all that she had undergone since she had left Mexico.

The fatigues of the voyage, however, in the hot summer, and the excessive labors which she felt it necessary to impose upon herself, were too much for the delicate organization of the Empress. She bore up under her sufferings with extraordinary fortitude, as long as any portion of the work, to which she had devoted herself, remained undone. But when she had accomplished her task, her energies gave way, and she was prostrated by a severe attack of sickness. In spite of all the care of her relatives and friends, this illness rapidly assumed an alarming character, and finally developed itself in brain fever of the most dangerous type. The highest medical talent in Europe was at once placed at her service, but for many weeks her life was despaired of. A merciful Providence however, watched over her, and at last her health was entirely restored.

In the meantime the situation in Mexico was becoming every month more embarrassing. In pursuance of the agreement made between the French government and the United States, the actual arrangements in Mexico, for the evacuation of Mexico by the French troops, were steadily progressing. Large bodies of French troops were withdrawn from distant points in the north and west of Mexico, and were concentrated at the capital, preparatory to marching to Vera Cruz, the point of embarkation. This left the States of Sonora, Chihuahua, Sinaloa, Durango, Coahuila, and part of New Leon, exposed to the incursions of the republican forces, whose ranks were in many cases augmented by bands of guerillas who joined them for the sake of the plunder of towns and villages. It would require a volume to relate the atrocities committed by these republican troops, at Hermosillo, at Ures, at Lajunta, at Sinoloa at Cosala, at Matamoras, at Mazatlan, and at dozens of smaller towns. Scarcely had the French troops been withdrawn from any place, before it would be entered by these Juarist troops, who, after first levying a forced contribution on the inhabitants, would then proceed to rob and plunder indiscriminately, and too often would indulge in outrages too gross for description.

It was at this critical juncture that the health of the Emperor gave way. His labors, for months past, had been excessive. His anxieties for the State had been very great. And now, when he most needed the presence and smiles of his beloved wife, came the crushing news of her dangerous illness. His first impulse, as a man and a husband, was to fly to her side. But when he understood the nature of her distressing malady, and that absolute quiet was essential to her recovery, he abandoned that idea. And this he did the more willingly, as he had full confidence in the skilful physicians by whom the Empress was attended; a confidence which the event has proved, was well founded. On the other hand, his duties as a sovereign, and the critical nature of the situation, absolutely required that he should remain in Mexico, at whatever sacrifice of his personal feelings. He bent all his energies, therefore, to the task before him. But his anxieties, his labors, and his cares, were too much even for the strongest constitution, and in October he was prostrated by a severe attack of fever. In November, when he had partially recovered, but while he was still very weak, he left the capital for a few days, and retired to Orizaba, where the air is pure and bracing, and where, the physicians thought, he might most speedily recover his strength. It was while he was at Orizaba, that the United States steamer Susquehanna arrived off Vera Cruz, with General Sherman and Mr. Campbell on board; and their mission to Mexico must now be explained.

The sending of General Sherman and Mr. Campbell to Vera Cruz, was unquestionably one of the greatest blunders in the history of modern diplomacy. Nothing was accomplished by the extraordinary step, except to place the United States in a ridiculous attitude before the world. The objects which Mr. Seward seems to have had in view were, 1st, to afford direct aid and encouragement to the Juarist party, which, of itself, would have been in violation of our pledge of neutrality; and, 2d, that General Sherman's presence at Vera Cruz might overawe the French officers in command, and cause them to hasten the embarkation of the French troops, under the guns of the frigate Susquehanna. The event shows that General Sherman's presence at Vera Cruz had just the contrary effect.

General Sherman and Mr. Campbell were sent to Vera Cruz under a misapprehension of existing facts which seems almost incredible. The situation in Mexico must have been perfectly well known to Mr. Seward, and yet his action seems to have been based upon two delusions: 1st, that General Sherman's presence at Vera Cruz would scare away the French; and 2d, that the empire and the present government of Mexico would fall, and the republic be restored in Mexico, immediately on the departure of the French troops.

Mr. Seward's instructions to Mr. Campbell were as follow:

"DEPARTMENT OF STATE,
"WASHINGTON, *Oct.* 20, 1866.

"SIR.—You are aware that a friendly and explicit arrangement exists between this government and the Emperor of France, to the effect that he will withdraw his expeditionary military forces from Mexico in three parts—the first of which shall leave Mexico in November next, the second in March next and the third in November, 1867, and that upon the evacuation being thus completed the French Government will immediately come upon the ground of non-intervention in regard to Mexico which is held by the United States. Doubts have been entertained and expressed in some quarters upon the question whether the French government will faithfully execute this agreement. No such doubts have been entertained by the President, who has had repeated and even recent assurances that the complete evacuation of Mexico by the French will be consummated at the periods mentioned, or earlier if compatible with climatical, military and other conditions. There are grounds for supposing that two incidental questions have already engaged the attention of the French government—namely, first, whether it should not advise the departure of the Prince Maximilian for Austria to be made before the withdrawal of the French expedition ; second, whether it would not be consistent with the climatical, military and other conditions before mentioned, to withdraw the whole expeditionary force at once, instead of retiring it in three separate instalments, and at different periods. No formal communication, however, upon this subject has been made by the Emperor Napoleon to the government of the United States. When the subject has been incidentally mentioned, this department, by direction of the President, has replied that the United States await the execution of the agreement for the evacuation by the government of France at least according to its letter, while they would be gratified if that agreement could be executed with greater promptness and dispatch than are stipulated. Under these circumstances the President expects that within the next month (November) a portion at least of the French expeditionary force will retire from Mexico, and he thinks it not improbable that the whole expeditionary force may be withdrawn at or about the same time. Such an event cannot fail to produce a crisis of great political interest in the republic of Mexico. It is important that you should be either within the territories of that republic or in some place near at hand, so as to assume the exercise of your functions as Minister Plenipotentiary of the United States to the republic of Mexico. What may be the proceedings of the Prince Maximilian in the event of a partial or complete evacuation of Mexico, of course cannot now be certainly foreseen. What may be the proceedings of Mr. Juarez, the President of the republic of Mexico, in the same event, cannot now be definitely anticipated. We are aware of the existence of several political parties in Mexico other than those at the head of which are President Juarez and Prince Maximilian, who entertain conflicting views concerning the most expedient and proper mode of restoring peace, order, and civil government in that republic. We do not know what may be the proceedings of those parties in the event of the French evacuation. Finally, it is impossible for us to foresee what may be the proceedings of the Mexican people in case of the happening of the events before alluded to. For these reasons it is impossible to give you specific directions for the conduct of your proceedings in the discharge of the high trust which the government of the United States has confided to you. Much must be left to your own discretion, which is to be exercised according to the view you may take of political movements as they shall disclose themselves in the future. There are, however, some principles which, as we think, may be safely laid down in regard to the policy which the government of the United States will expect you to pursue. The first of these is that, as a representative of the United States, you are accredited to the republican government of Mexico, of which Mr. Juarez is President. Your communications as such representative will be made to him, wheresoever he may be, and in no event will you officially recognize either the Prince Maximilian, who claims to be Emperor, or any other person, chief, or combination, as exercising the executive authority in Mexico, without having first reported to this department, and received instructions from the President of the United States. Secondly, assuming that the French military and naval commanders shall be engaged in good faith in executing the agreement before mentioned for the evacuation of Mexico, the spirit of the engagement on our part in relation to that event will forbid the United States and their representative from obstructing or embarrassing the departure of the French. Thirdly, what the government of the United States desires in regard to the future of Mexico is not the conquest of Mexico, or any part of it, or the aggrandizement of the United States by purchases of land or dominion, but, on the other hand, they desire to see the people of Mexico relieved from all foreign military intervention, to the end that they may resume the conduct of their own affairs under the existing republican government, or such other form of government as, being left in the enjoyment of perfect liberty, they shall determine to adopt in the exercise of their own free will, by their own act, without dictation from any foreign country, and of course without dictation from the United States. It results, as a consequence from these principles, that you will enter into no stipulation with the French commanders, or with the Prince Maximilian, or with any other party, which shall have a tendency to counteract or oppose the administration of President Juarez, or to hinder or delay the restoration of the authority of the republic. On the other hand, it may possibly happen that the President of the republic of Mexico may desire the good offices of the United States, or even some effective proceedings on our part, to favor and advance the pacification of a country so long distracted by foreign combined with civil war, and thus gain time for the re-establishment of national authority upon principles consistent with a republican and domestic system of government. It is possible, moreover, that some disposition might be made of the land and naval forces of the United States without interfering within the jurisdiction of Mexico, or violating the laws of neutrality, which would be useful in favoring the restoration of law, order, and republican government in that country. You are authorized to confer upon this subject with the republican government of Mexico and its agents, and also to confer informally, if you find it necessary, with any other parties or agents, should such an exceptional conference become absolutely necessary, but not otherwise. You will by these means obtain information which will be important to this government, and such information you will convey to this department, with your suggestions and advice as to any proceedings on our part which can be adopted in conformity with the principles I have before laid down. You will be content with thus referring any important propositions on the subject of reorganization and restoration of the republican government in Mexico as may arise to this department, for the information of the President. The Lieutenant-General of the United States possesses already discretionary authority as to the location of the forces of the United States in the vicinity of Mexico. His military experience will enable him to advise you concerning such questions as may arise during the transition stage of Mexico from a state of military siege by a foreign enemy to a condition of practical self-government. At the same time it will be in his power, being near the scene of action, to issue any orders which may be expedient or necessary for maintaining the obligations resting upon the United States in regard to proceedings upon the borders of Mexico. For these reasons he has been requested and instructed by the President to proceed with you to your destination, and act with you as an adviser, recognized by this department, in regard to the matters which have been herein discussed. After conferring with him, you are at liberty to proceed to the City of Chihuahua, or to such other place in Mexico as may be the residence of President Juarez; or, in your discretion, you will proceed to any other place in Mexico not held or occupied at the time of your arrival by enemies of the republic of Mexico; or you will stop at any place in the United States or elsewhere, near the frontier or coast of Mexico; and await there a time to enter any portion of Mexico which shall hereafter be in the occupation of the republican government of Mexico.

"I am, sir, your obedient servant,

"WILLIAM H. SEWARD.

"LEWIS D. CAMPBELL, etc."

In pursuance of these instructions, General Sherman and Mr. Campbell sailed from New York about the 10th of November, and after spending a few days at Havana, in order to learn some reliable news of the real condition of affairs in Mexico, arrived off Vera Cruz on the evening of the 29th. The vessel remained there until the midnight following, Sunday, December 2, when she sailed away under cover of the darkness of the night, and thus ended the Sherman and Campbell mission to Mexico. Mr. Campbell found the situation in Mexico to be such that he could not carry out his instructions. General Sherman found that if he had been sent there to watch the embarkation of the French, some months must elapse before he could enjoy that pleasing spectacle. The Susquehanna therefore made the best of her way to New Orleans, where she arrived about the 8th of December, touching at Tampico and Matamoras on the way.

A well-informed correspondent of the "New York Herald," writing from Washington, gives the follow ing facts in relation to the affair:—

"Mexican advices state that the abortive Susquehanna expedition has proved a positive injury to the Juarez government. The Mexicans are in nothing so consistent as in their jealous hatred of all foreigners. Had Sherman and Campbell succeeded in reaching Juarez, it is doubtful whether their presence in the republican seat of government under existing circumstances would not have been more a source of weakness than of strength to the Mexican President. As it is, their failure to do any thing at all has cast ridicule upon the United States; has drawn upon Juarez the suspicion of trafficking with the foreigner, and has given the cause of Ortega, who is looked upon as the anti-American candidate for the presidency, an impetus which would otherwise have been wanting. Minister Campbell is understood to complain that Juarez made no effort to communicate with the embassy, and rather thwarted than aided their feeble attempts to communicate with him. Juarez probably had a deep meaning in holding aloof from emissaries who came without power to afford him actual assistance, and whose presence at his head-quarters would compromise him with his countrymen.

"There are some piquant little facts connected with the expedition which have never yet been told. Sherman and Campbell pulled together from the start like a baulky team. Each had separate instructions, and each claimed to rank the other. On the arrival of the Susquehanna at Vera Cruz, Sherman, it seems, was for accepting Bazaine's invitation and going straight to

Mexico city. Campbell strongly opposed the suggestion on the ground that he was accredited to Juarez only, and had nothing to do with Bazaine, Castelnau, or any one outside the republic of Mexico. This argument at last prevailed; but not till after a somewhat stormy discussion, in the course of which personal allusions to kid-gloved aides-de-camp and legation secretaries presumed to be "on the make" had been pretty freely interchanged. The breach thus occasioned was never healed, and culminated at Matamoras in Sherman returning to New Orleans by the Susquehanna and Campbell by private steamer. Sherman took up his quarters with Sheridan in New Orleans, and Campbell buried himself in the fourth story of an indifferent hotel, each speaking contemptuously of the other and giving a contradictory account of the expedition."

There is no doubt of the substantial correctness of this statement. The "Herald" itself, in speaking of it, says:—

"THE CAMPBELL-SHERMAN MISSION—MAXIMILIAN SAYS HE WILL DIE WHERE HE IS.

"Our Washington despatches give us the latest account of the inside history of the late Sherman-Campbell mission to Mexico, which is so interesting as to merit a few words from us. Two prominent facts are revealed —one, that the mission did not do the work intended for it;* and the other, that Juarez made no attempt to

* The "Herald" adds here, "because the elements composing it were inharmonious,"—which was *not* the cause of its failure.

hold any communication with the members of that commission because he feared to arouse the jealous susceptibility of his countrymen. The case, then, thus stated, presents a rather unexpected aspect; for, putting aside for a moment the unchemical compound known as the Campbell-Sherman mission, we are informed in plain terms that the Mexican people fear any action our government may take toward restoring the republican form of government among them from a deep-rooted conviction that we are impelled thereto by interested motives. Direct allusion to this was made by Juarez in his speech at Chihuahua, when he expressed a hope that the United States does not think of annexing any portion of Mexican territory. We have repeatedly disclaimed any such intention, but it is very doubtful if our declarations have had the slightest effect toward removing the deep distrust entertained of us in Mexico. The greater the pity, therefore, that the Campbell-Sherman mission exploded as it did. That commission not only covered itself with ridicule and threw discredit on the United States government in the eyes of the Mexicans, but an opportunity was lost for removing the delusion which that entire nation persists in adhering to. Minister Campbell may or may not have been the proper person for the business. We are strongly inclined to think he was totally unfit. General Sherman may or may not have been the right man; but one thing is very plain—that each considered himself the head of the mission, and, as is the case in all unnatural things with two heads, the thing was a monster and died after a brief, unhealthy existence.

"Another curious feature in our latest Mexican news is the reported conversation between General Castelnau and Maximilian, wherein the former is said to have urged an abdication, while the latter announced his determination to remain where he is till he dies."

But what was the effect of this mission in Mexico? The New Orleans "Picayune," of December 13, says:—

"The news which we publish this afternoon puts an entirely new light upon affairs in Mexico. It would seem that the alliance between Juarez and the United States, the reported sale of Mexican territory, movements on the border and expedition of the Susquehannah, with General Sherman and Minister Campbell to Mexican waters, have frightened the Mexicans into their usual liberality, when the integrity of their country is feared. The church, always the first to move, have placed $25,000,000 at the disposal of the Emperor, and the merchants have promised to give him $10,000,000 annually, provided he will remain. To this proposition he assented, immediately issued his proclamation accordingly, and the empire is, for the time being, re-established."

"This has given great joy throughout the country. Church bells were rung, bonfires lighted, and a large mass of the people went into ecstacies of joy. A new impulse was at once given also to works of internal improvement, railroads, telegraphs, etc."

The fact is, on recovering from his sickness, the Emperor Maximilian found that the difficulties surrounding him were very great; but, on a candid consideration of them, he did not deem them insuperable. General Castelnau, who had recently arrived from Paris, presented to him the alternative of abdication: but this proposal did not commend itself to the Emperor with any degree of favor. After having devoted all the energies of his life, for three years, to the great work of making of Mexico a happy and prosperous country, Maximilian did not think that this was the time to abandon all that he had done, and to leave the country to anarchy. He convoked the council of ministers therefore, and after laying before them a candid statement of the difficulties of the situation, he desired their frank opinion, whether there was any existing reason, why he ought to abdicate? Their unanimous reply was, that by all means he ought to remain at the head of the government. As this fully coincided with his own views, there was no further question about the matter, and the following proclamations were at once issued:—

"PROCLAMATION OF THE PREFECT OF VERA CRUZ.
VERA CRUZ, *Dec.* 1, 1866.

Viva el Emperio! Viva el Emperador! Vera Cruzanos! One of the greatest events for the good Mexicans has happened to give renewed life to the nation. His majesty the Emperor, who has made so many sacrifices for the well being and happiness of our dear country, has given the final proof of his consideration for our welfare while agitated by those natural sentiments which struggled in his breast. In consequence of the affliction of his august and noble spouse, our lovely sovereign, it was for a moment feared that he would temporarily quit the country to dedicate his whole time to the rendering of those attentions, which the delicate state of health of his worthy consort rendered necessary. But the Emperor has sacrificed all for us, has put aside his duties as a man for those which concern his house as a ruler, and in the momentous crisis now overhanging the country declares solemnly his intention of continuing in the front, even to the extent of shedding the last drop of his blood in the defence of the nation. Citizens of Vera Cruz, we congratulate you. Let us give thanks to Providence for having saved the integrity of our country, and from the inmost recesses of our hearts let us hail the day of resurrection of our nationality, which was on the eve of being destroyed.

"PROCLAMATION OF THE EMPEROR MAXIMILIAN.

"MEXICANS.—Circumstances of great magnitude relating to the welfare of our country, and which increase in strength by our domestic difficulties, have produced in our mind the conviction that we ought to reconsider the power confided to us.

"Our Council of Ministers, by us convoked, has given as their opinion that the welfare of Mexico still requires our presence at the head of affairs, and we have considered it our duty to accede to their request. We announce at the same time our intention to convoke a national Congress on the most ample and liberal basis, where all political parties can participate. This Congress shall decide whether the empire shall continue in future, and in case of assent, shall assist in framing the fundamental laws to consolidate the public institutions of the country; to obtain this result our counsellors are at present engaged in devising the necessary means, and at the same time arrange matters in such a manner that all parties may assist in an arrangement on that basis.

"In the meantime, Mexicans, counting upon you all, without excluding any political class, we shall continue with courage and constancy, the work of regeneration which you have placed in charge of your countryman

"MAXIMILIAN.

"ORIZABA, *Dec.* 1, 1866."

In taking this step the chief reliance of the Emperor Maximilian was upon the Mexican people themselves. The events of December, 1866, and of January and February, 1867, have demonstrated that this confidence was not misplaced. The Mexican people seemed to appreciate the gravity of the situation, and they rallied around the Emperor, determined to uphold him, and the government which he had administered with such wisdom and paternal care. All classes rushed to his support. The clergy and the merchants furnished the financial means that were necessary for immediate use; volunteers flocked to the army, and swelled the ranks of the regiments; and soon all matters began to wear an encouraging aspect. The Sherman and Cambell mission therefore, so far from witnessing the downfall of the Mexican Empire, has only demonstrated the attachment of the Mexican people to it, and their determination to uphold it.

Military operations against the Juarists' were at once commenced, and were carried on with vigor and success. Ortega, the legal President of the defunct Mexican republic, escaping from the illegal imprisonment to which he had been subjected by General Sheridan, had crossed the Rio Grande, and his partisans and those of Juarez were at once engaged in deadly strife with each other. The latest intelligence from Mexico brings us the news of the capture of the cities of Zacatecas and San Luis Potosi, by a Division of the Imperial troops under the Mexican General Miramon, —the defeat of the republican troops at those points, and the capture of Juarez himself.

The fate of Mexico depends upon the United States. If our neutrality toward that country is maintained, in accordance with Mr. Seward's promise to the Emperor Napoleon, the "republican" faction in Mexico will destroy each other, and the government under Maximilian will become firmly established. But it may be quite another matter if we continue to take the part of the usurper Juarez against the legal President Ortega, and if the Juarists continue to derive aid and encouragement from the United States. In consequence of such intervention, Maximilian may be forced to abdicate: and what will be the result then? The war between the Juarists and the followers of Ortega will rage with greater bitterness than ever: Mexico will at once revert to its former condition of anarchy: and continual civil wars will absorb all the energies and all the wealth of the people. Mexico has never prospered under a republic, and the history and character of her people proves that she never can prosper under that form of government. To re-establish the republic in Mexico would simply be to give up that country to the pillage of rival republican chiefs.

Under such a state of things, every foreign nation which has claims against Mexico would at once present them, and Mexico would again be at the mercy of every foreign power. England, Spain, and France, all have heavy claims against Mexico, which remain unsatisfied to this day. Under the present government of that country, there is a fair prospect that those claims will be eventually paid. France has arranged for hers, and England and Spain are willing to wait.

But the matter would be very different, if the present government of Mexico should be destroyed by intervention on the part of the United States; and with it, the ability of Mexico to satisfy these claims. Those three nations would again make war upon Mexico, as they did in 1861: they would be compelled to do so, in order to obtain for their own citizens the payment of their just claims. The end of such a war would find Mexico dismembered, as we dismembered her at the end of our Mexican war in 1848. The Isthmus of Tehuantepec, with its already surveyed railroad between the Atlantic and Pacific Ocean, and the States of Oaxaca, Tabaso, Chiapas, Campeche, and Yucatan, lie very convenient to the British and Spanish possessions in the Balize and Cuba: and nothing would be easier than for the French, at the same time, to again occupy and hold the port and State of Vera Cruz, and the city of Mexico, with the immediately surrounding country.

The best and richest half of Mexico thus disposed of, what would become of the remainder? It would ultimately be absorbed by the United States, and Mexico, as a nation, would disappear from the face of the earth.

CHAPTER VIII.

Policy of the United States toward Mexico—Question before the "Lincoln Administration: "Shall we Save the Mexican Republic?"—Consequences to the North of Interference in Opposition to Napoleon—Object of the American Civil War—Interference with the Emperor Napoleon would Defeat that Object—Critical Condition of the North in 1862—Consequences to the North if the Emperor Napoleon should Recognize the South—The United States Determine to Maintain a Neutral Policy—The United States Government Acknowledges the Right of France to make War on the Mexican Republic, and to Secure the Fruits of Victory.

No sooner did the Emperor Maximilian ascend the throne of Mexico, than he communicated the fact of his accession to all the great powers of the world, and among the rest, to the United States. This was in May, 1864. The United States government took no notice of the communication. All the other great powers immediately recognized the empire of Mexico, sent ministers to reside at the court of Maximilian, and received ministers from him to reside at their capitals. But why did the United States not interfere in time to prevent the extinction of the Mexican republic?

When France made war on Mexico, in 1861 and 1862; when the French expedition, under General

Forey, was sent to Mexico, the United States was invited to join that expedition. The United States government declined, but at the same time admitted the justice of the war on the part of France. On the 11th of September, 1863, Mr. Seward said to Mr. Motley, our minister to Vienna: "When France made war against Mexico, we asked of France explanations of her objects and purposes. She answered that it was a war for the redress of grievances; that she did not intend to permanently occupy or dominate in Mexico; and that she should leave to the people of Mexico a free choice of institutions of government. Under these circumstances the United States adopted, and they have since maintained, entire neutrality between the belligerents, in harmony with our traditional policy in regard to foreign wars."

But our policy toward Mexico had a deeper foundation than that. At the time of the French intervention in Mexico, the United States were engaged in civil war. In 1862, when it became necessary for our government to decide what our policy toward Mexico was to be—when it became absolutely necessary for us to decide whether we would uphold the Monroe doctrine in Mexico, and save the republic there, or remain coldly looking on while the empire was being established—at that time matters did not look well for the North.

The first war fever had passed away, and people

began to realize that they had been entrapped into a job that was going to be any thing but an easy one. Drafting had not yet begun, but it was plainly seen that conscription was inevitable, and that without forced conscription the war could not be carried on. It was plainly seen that the real object of the war was to free the negroes and to subjugate the Southern States; and that in giving liberty to the blacks the white people would lose their own.

The finances of the country had begun to get deranged. All the specie in the country had been withdrawn from circulation, and had been sent to Europe to buy arms; and our new national bank-note currency had not yet got under headway. The events of the war had not been such as to inspire confidence as to the result of the struggle. The North had been defeated, and the South had been victorious, at Big Bethel, Bull Run, Manassas Junction, Ball's Bluff, and Belmont. Washington had been beleaguered by the Confederate forces, from the battle of Manassas, in July, 1861, until March, 1862, a period of seven months. President Lincoln had offered the South four hundred millions of dollars for the liberation of their slaves, and the offer had been refused. The peninsula campaign against Richmond had not been successful. The national army had then been placed under the command of General Pope. It had been defeated with terrible loss, and had retreated in confusion to Washington, at the end of August, 1862; and the prestige of General McClellan's name alone had saved the capital from capture. The President had left the White House, so imminent was the danger, and had gone to General McClellan's residence, and implored him to take command of all the troops for the defence of the capital; and a locomotive was kept at the depot, with steam up day and night, ready to convey Mr. Lincoln and Mr. Stanton away to Baltimore in case the Confederates should attack Washington.

Such was the situation, when Mr. Lincoln was called upon to adopt a course of policy toward Mexico. And here it must be remembered who caused the war, and for what purpose it was waged. The war originated in a systematic conspiracy on the part of the leaders of the radical Republican party, of whom Mr. Lincoln was one, for the conquest and subjugation of the Southern States. Any person with a calm and unprejudiced mind, who will sit down and study the political history of the country for the last forty years, can plainly trace this conspiracy through the whole of that long period. It took its rise in that spirit of intolerance which has always been the distinguishing trait of New England Puritanism. This spirit of intolerance had swept all over the Northern States, and wherever it could make its influence felt, it compelled men to abandon the most cherished convictions of their lives, and to conform to the rigid, unbending standard of Puritan morality and politics.

The conspiracy was successful in driving the Southern States to secede, so as to have a pretext for making war on them. It was also successful in exciting the North to make war on them, by pretending that it should be a war for the restoration of the Union. Left alone, there was a possibility that the North, after a war of some years' duration, might subjugate the Southern States and impose upon them whatever conditions they pleased. But it was certain that the North could not conquer the Southern States if any European power should recognize the latter as an independent government and enter into an alliance with them. And there seemed reason to fear that this would take place. England was building magnificent iron-clad vessels for the South; and all through Mr. Seward's diplomatic correspondence, in 1862, are expressions of fear that the Emperor Napoleon might recognize the South.

One or two instances of this must suffice here for illustration. On the 15th of September, 1863, the Minister of Foreign Affairs wrote as follows to the French minister at Washington:

"PARIS, *September* 15, 1863.

"Mr. Dayton, the American minister, has been moved at certain rumors which appear lately to have obtained some credit at Paris, and he has come to converse with me about them. According to these reports, the Emperor's government has decided to recognize the Southern States, and a treaty has even been already signed, according to which the new confederacy is to cede to France, Texas and a part of Louisiana."

On the 9th of October, 1863, Mr. Seward wrote to Mr. Dayton, our minister to France:

"We know from many sources, and even from the direct statement of the Emperor of France, that on the breaking out of the insurrection he adopted the then current opinion of European statesmen that the efforts of this government to suppress it would be unsuccessful. To this pre-judgment we attribute his agreement with Great Britain to act in concert with her upon international questions which might arise out of the conflict, his practical concession of a belligerent character to the insurgents, his repeated suggestions of accommodations by this government with the insurgents, *and his conferences on the subject of a recognition.* These proceedings of the Emperor of France have been very injurious to the United States by encouraging and thus prolonging the insurrection. When recurring *to what the Emperor of France has already done,* we cannot, at any time, feel assured that, under mistaken impressions of our embarrassments in consequence of a lamentable civil war, he may not *go further in the way of encouragement to the insurgents,* whose intrigues in Paris we understand and do not under-estimate."

Of course, if the Emperor Napoleon should "go much further in the way of encouragement to the insurgents" than "he had already done;" if "his conferences on the subject of recognition" should lead him finally to recognize the South, then the grand conspiracy of the radical Republicans, for the conquest and subjugation of the Southern States, to which Mr. Lincoln was fully committed, would have to be abandoned. What, then, was to be done?

There was Napoleon, making war against Mexico, just as we, said the radical Republicans, are making war against the South. If we interfere, we shall save the Mexican republic, save Mexico from conquest, baffle all of Napoleon's designs. If Napoleon interposes in our quarrel, he will save the cause for which the South is fighting, will save the South from conquest, will baffle all our designs. If we let Napoleon alone, he can do what he pleases in Mexico. If we can induce Napoleon to let us alone, we can do what we please with the Southern States.

Thus Mr. Lincoln and the radical Republicans reasoned, in 1862; and thus it was that no hand on our part was raised to save the Mexican republic or to vindicate the Monroe doctrine. This is the key to the whole policy of the United States toward Mexico, from 1861 to 1866. The Washington correspondent of the "New York News," in a letter dated Washington, December 30th, 1865, says:

How the North Conquered the South.

"It is a great mistake to suppose, or to say, that the diplomatic correspondence of our government with France, in regard to Mexican affairs, when it is sent in to Congress, 'will show that our government has at no time had any purpose or thought of abandoning the Monroe doctrine.' On the other hand, that correspondence will show that the Monroe doctrine was abandoned by the government, in 1861 and 1862, when Napoleon first began the execution of his designs in Mexico, and communicated those designs to us. The government clearly perceived at that time that if we declared our firm determination then to uphold the Monroe doctrine, and not to permit the establishment of a monarchy in Mexico, that Napoleon would recognize the Southern Confederacy, and would then, after assisting the South to gain her independence, establish a monarchy in Mexico and enter into an alliance with the Southern Confederacy. The proofs of this are scattered all through Mr. Dayton's diplomatic correspondence, in 1862 and 1863; while, on the other hand, if we yielded to what seemed a military necessity, gave a tacit consent to Napoleon's operations against Mexico, and said nothing about the Monroe doctrine, we would thereby secure Napoleon's neutrality and would be able to conquer the South. I assert, and I defy contradiction, that this alternative was considered at several successive Cabinet meetings, in the fall and winter of 1861, and that the latter was deliberately chosen. It was deliberately decided by the government that the Monroe doctrine should be sacrificed, in order that we might be able to 'whip the South.' We see the result to-day in the firm establishment of the Mexican empire, a result which the government must have foreseen. The only alternative left to us now is to recognize that empire, or to go to war with France, Austria, Belgium, Spain, Italy, and England, in order to root it out. The idea that Maximilian will abdicate, or that he will be deserted by his European allies, is too preposterous to be noticed."

On the 26th of September, 1863, Mr. Seward wrote to Mr. Dayton, our minister to Paris: "The United States have neither the right nor the disposition to intervene by force on either side, in the war which is going on between France and Mexico." On the eleventh of the same month, he wrote to Mr. Motley, our minister to Austria: "When France made war against Mexico, we asked of France explanations of her objects and purposes. She answered, that it was a war for the redress of grievances; and that she did not intend permanently to occupy or dominate in Mexico, and that she should leave to the people of Mexico a free choice of institutions of government. Under these circumstances the United States adopted, and they have since maintained, entire neutrality between the belligerents, in harmony with the traditional policy in regard to foreign wars.

CHAPTER IX.

Policy of President Johnson's Administration toward Mexico—His Message in December, 1865—Our Policy to be Based upon the Principle of Non-Intervention—We must Finally Recognize the Government de Facto—Why Mr. Logan was Appointed Minister to Mexico—Why he Refused the Appointment—Why Mr. Campbell was Appointed—Why Mr. Campbell is Not Permitted to go to Mexico—No Constitutional Republican Government in Mexico in Existence—Juarez a Usurper.

THE policy of the United States toward Mexico, from 1861 to 1865, might have been right or wrong. President Johnson had nothing to do with it. On his accession to the Presidency, he found that the republic of Mexico no longer existed, and that it had been succeeded by an empire which was firmly established, and which had been formally recognized by the eight great powers of the earth. He found, that of all the great powers of the earth, the United States was the only one that was not holding diplomatic relations with Mexico. He found, that for the first time in our history, the United States had failed to recognize a de facto government. On further inquiry and study, he found it to be an unquestionable fact that the new government in Mexico had been established by the will of the people, and was heartily supported by nine tenths of the population of Mexico, including all the honest and industrious people, all the merchants, all the men of wealth and property, all the educated and professional men, and by the church. He found that it was opposed solely by a few bands of guerillas.

The question for him to determine was, whether he should interpose and uproot all this, and, by forcing a republican government upon Mexico, throw back that country into its former condition of anarchy and weakness, or whether, on the other hand, he should observe our settled policy of non-intervention in the affairs of other nations, and leave Mexico to the enjoyment of that government which she had chosen, and under which, for three years, her people had been so happy and prosperous.

The Washington correspondent of the New York "News," in his letter of December 8, 1865, in speaking of the message which President Johnson had just sent in to Congress, says:

"There is nothing either in the character of Andrew Johnson, or in the circumstances by which he is surrounded, which require him to use the language of ambiguity in speaking of the relations in which we stand toward Mexico. If the government intends to uphold the Monroe doctrine in Mexico, there is no reason why the President should not plainly say so. But he does not say it, nor can any such intention be implied from what he does say. Napoleon has done a certâin work in Mexico. What he has done there is finished and complete. There is nothing more for him to do there. But the whole world knows what he has done: namely, that he has established in Mexico a strong and permanent government. Now, if Mr. Johnson objected to that; if he objected to what Napoleon has done in Mexico; if he intended to take any measures to undo what Napoleon has done; if he intended to take any measures whatever for the expulsion of Maximilian and the resuscitation of the Mexican republic, he would have said so, plainly and unequivocally, in his message. But he says nothing of the kind. He does not complain of or object to, any thing that Napoleon has done in Mexico. He does say, in a very vague and indefinite manner, that we might protect ourselves against designs inimical to our own government; but he does not say that the government has any design to interfere in favor of a republic in Mexico. On the contrary, alluding to the fact that the Mexicans seem to have chosen a monachy instead of a republic, he says, that "Republicanism is the only government suited to our condition; but we have never sought to impose it upon others."

"INTENTIONS OF THE GOVERNMENT TOWARD MEXICO.

"Again, in the whole Message there is not one word of sympathy for the Mexican republic; not one word of regret that the republic has fallen, and has been succeeded by an empire; not one word of encouragement to Juarez and his followers. This studied omission must mean something. It can only mean that the government does not feel any such sympathy or regret. Mr. Johnson is not the man to suppress the sentiments of the government on such a subject. A correspondence between the United States and France, on the subject, is alluded to. We are not left in the dark as to the nature of that correspondence. Napoleon's designs in regard to Mexico have been plainly and unequivocally expressed, and have been before the world ever since 1863. He concealed nothing from the first. The purpose which he had in view, and which was announced as early as 1863, has been fully accomplished. There is nothing more in Mexico for him to do; and he has no 'designs,' 'inimical' or otherwise, 'toward the United States,' or 'against our government.' He has even offered to withdraw from Mexico all the French troops, if we will maintain our former neutrality toward Mexico. On our part, the correspondence alluded to by the President has been carried on by Mr. Seward. Mr. Seward is not a man whose foreign policy is subject to sudden changes. We have Mr. Seward's diplomatic correspon. dence down to the end of the year 1864. We have his letters to all of our foreign ministers long after the empire in Mexico was firmly established, and his instructions to them on that subject. There is no ambiguity in those letters. He speaks plainly and to the point. And the whole tenor of what he says is this: that, under no circumstances, will the United States interfere in what is going on in Mexico; that we will continue to preserve the most perfect neutrality between the belligerents, and that in the end we will recognize the government which shall be finally established."

The same writer, in another letter of the same date, says, in relation to the appointment of Mr. Logan as minister to the *republic* of Mexico:—

"General Logan arrived here last evening, and had an interview with the President and Secretary of State before the cabinet meeting to-day. He stated to the President that he would gladly accept the post of minister to Mexico, if the government would assure him that our policy toward Mexico would be changed, and that we would aid the liberals in Mexico in expelling Maximilian and in restoring the republic; but that he positively declined the mission until he should receive such assurances. The President informed him that he could not give him those assurances; that, up to this time, the government had not determined to make any change in its policy, Mr. Seward added that non-interference in the affairs of other nations was one of the fundamental principles of our government; that, so far as it applied to Mexico, that policy had been adopted when France made war against Mexico, in 1861, and had been steadily adhered to ever since; and there was no reason for a departure from that policy now; that it would, on the other hand, be maintained and continued; that the Mexican people must be left free to decide their form of government for themselves; that, as the President had stated in his message, "we have never been the propagandists of republicanism, and have never sought to impose our form of government upon others;" and that we must recognize the sovereignty of Mexico in whatever form the Mexican people themselves choose to manifest it.

"Thus the matter ended; and thus ends the delusion that the American people indulged in when the appointment of General Logan was first announced."

The same writer, in a letter to the "Chicago Times" dated December 24, 1865, thus explains the subsequent appointment of Mr. Campbell, in place of Mr. Logan:—

"The appointment of Mr. Campbell is a tub thrown to the whale. It was made from the same motives, and with the same end in view, as Mr. Logan's appointment. Our foreign affairs under this administration, are managed exclusively by Mr. Seward, precisely the same as they were under the former administration. Mr. Seward sees the necessity of making some concession to the strong feeling in favor of the Monroe doctrine, which has recently found such emphatic expression in Congress; and therefore he caused Mr. Campbell to be appointed in place of Mr. Logan, who declined. But the appointment of Mr. Campbell is not the fact upon which the public should fix their attention. The great point to be ascertained is, why did General Logan refuse to accept the Mexican mission? That is the important point; and on this point the readers of the "Times" shall not be in the dark.

General Logan was appointed November 14, 1865. He was selected because he had identified himself with the Monroe doctrine and was prominently before the public as an advocate for its enforcement, even by force of arms, if necessary. The Democratic press everywhere throughout the country hailed his appointment, as affording a sure indication that our policy toward Mexico would be changed, and that our government intended now to take an active stand in favor of the Mexican republic. General Logan himself believed so. But I ascertained, and stated before the end of that month, that he was mistaken, and that, when he discovered that fact, he would refuse to accept the mission. The event has confirmed this statement. On the 8th inst., he had a long interview with the President and Secretary of State. For some days previously Mr. Seward had been urging him to accept the appointment. The time had now come when he must decide. He frankly expressed his desire to go to Mexico, if he could be assured that our policy toward that country would be changed. But he declared his unwillingness to go, unless the government intended to extend some substantial aid to the liberals. He was informed that our policy of neutrality toward Mexico would remain unchanged for the present, and he at once and peremptorily refused the mission. What transpired at this interview was kept a profound secret for ten days, and in the meantime, the public was informed almost daily that General Logan would probably accept. But, on the 21st inst., the "Intelligencer" announced the appointment of Mr. Campbell 'in place of Mr. Logan who declines.'

"Now who can believe that the policy of the administration, on an important question of foreign policy like this, has changed since the 8th of December? Depend upon it, that policy is unchanged. But Mr. Campbell is a different man from General Logan. I believe him to be a man of ability, and a gentleman who would not disgrace the diplomatic service of the country. But he is not particularly distinguished as 'a Monroe doctrine man,' and his appointment does not carry the weight that Mr. Logan's did. And he was spoken of, only a few weeks ago, by an able and usually accurate Washington correspondent as a hanger-around bar-rooms and saloons, and as a man who had already outlived his influence. What is the precise nature of his instructions, and what his course will be, I am as yet unable to say. Your readers may be assured, however, on two points: 1. That there is nothing in his instructions which will lead the liberals in Mexico to expect any aid from the United States, or that will bring about hostilities between the United States and France; and, 2. That the reasons which impel the United States to appoint a minister to the Mexican republic are so well understood at Paris that this appointment will not affect the diplomatic relations between the United States and France."

Our policy of neutrality toward Mexico is based upon sound principles of international law. The

United States government, in 1862, acknowledged the right of France to resort to war in order to enforce her just claims against Mexico. That acknowledgment was of itself an engagement on the part of the United States to recognize any de facto government that might be the legitimate result of that war. See Wheaton's International Law, Lawrence's edition. That the government of the United States intended that such a government de facto in Mexico should eventually be recognized, is evident from Mr. Seward's diplomatic correspondence.

THE TREATY WITH PRESIDENT JUAREZ.

But there are deeper and more important considerations, even than these, which require a brief historical retrospect. In accordance with the Mexican constitution Juarez was elected President in 1859. In 1860 our minister to Mexico negotiated a treaty with him, which would have been vastly advantageous to us in a commercial point of view, and would, in all probability, have prevented the subsequent intervention by England and France, and the present establishment of the Mexican empire.

By this treaty the Mexican government granted the right of way for railroad purposes, through the States of Sonora and Chihuahua, with a protectorate over the same; in consideration of which the United States agreed to loan Juarez four million dollars. What would have been the result of the ratification of this treaty? In the first place, it would have firmly established the constitutional republican government of Mexico, under President Juarez. It would have enabled the latter to have paid off the foreign debts of Mexico, thus taking away all pretence for subsequent French interference; and, finally, it would have enabled the Mexican people to demonstrate whether or not they were capable of living under a republican government. Besides that it would have given us an opportunity, and the means of building a Southern Pacific Railroad, running through Texas, with its western terminus at the seaport of Guaymas. Suppose the four million dollars had never been repaid, what then? We would have a protectorate over the whole of the two northern States of Mexico. They would already be in our possession, and they would, ultimately, have been ceded to the United States.

WHY WAS THE TREATY NOT RATIFIED?

That treaty, however, failed to receive the ratification of the Senate. It is true that this treaty pledged the United States to uphold the Monroe doctrine (as it was then understood, and as it has been until now understood) in Mexico. Was that the reason why it was not ratified? Whatever the reason was, the refusal of the Senate to ratify this treaty, prepared the way for the downfall of the Mexican republic, and opened the way for the establishment of the empire.

Three years have elapsed since the establishment of the Mexican empire. Its stability seems to be beyond question. Can it be possible that a nation of eight millions of people would have permitted this state of things if they were, indeed, opposed to it? It has been a favorite expression that the throne of Maximilian is upheld by French bayonets. But that is not true in the sense that it is intended. It is true that the Mexican empire is upheld by the moral force of France. But at any time during the last eighteen months it has been within the power of the Mexican nation to expel Maximilian and restore Juarez and the republican government, if the Mexican people really wished to do so. But what have they done? What has this nation of eight millions of people done? They have seen Juarez driven from Mexico to San Luis Potosi, from San Luis to Chihuahua, from Chihuahua to El Paso del Norte. From fifty thousand troops which he had when the French began the siege of Puebla, his forces have dwindled down to twenty thousand, to ten thousand, to four thousand, and at last to a few bands of scattered guerillas and robbers. Would the Mexican nation have permitted this if they really wished a republic?

WHY HAVE WE NOT ASSISTED MEXICO?

It is true they have been disappointed in not receiving from the United States that assistance in their struggle which they felt they had a right to look for from a powerful sister republic, contiguous to their own. Why was this? When Juarez fled from Mexico to San Luis, in June, 1863, he invited our Minister Mr. Corwin, to go with him. Mr. Corwin declined, and Mr. Seward wrote to him on the 8th of August, 1863, that the President approved of his decision in so declining. Since that time we have not even pretended to maintain any diplomatic relations with the republican government of Mexico in that country. Appeal after appeal has been made by Juarez for aid, but the United States Government has maintained a cold and studied indifference. On the 15th of December, 1862, Mr. Seward wrote to M. Romero: "The United States laments the war which has arisen between the republic of Mexico and France. Since it has unhappily occurred, however, they can act in regard to it only on the principles which have always governed their conduct in similar cases." In other words, we would recognize the government de facto, by whichever party it might be in the end established. On the 26th of September, 1863, Mr. Seward wrote to our Minister at the Austrian Court: "The events which are occurring in Mexico are regarded as incidents of the war between France and Mexico" (the French were then in possession of the Mexican capital, and the crown had been offered to an Austrian Prince). On the 23d of October, 1863, Mr. Seward wrote to our minister in England that Maximilian had declared his willingness to accept the imperial throne in Mexico if he shall be called to it by the voice of the Mexican nation; and concludes his dispatch by saying: "The United States can do no otherwise than leave the destinies of Mexico in the keeping of her own people, and recognize their sovereignty and independence in whatever form they themselves shall choose that this sovereignty and independence shall be manifested." On the 26th of September, 1863, Mr. Seward also wrote to Mr. Dayton: "The United States have neither the right nor the disposition to intervene by force, on either side, in the lamentable war which is going on between France and Mexico. They have neither a right nor a disposition to intervene by force in the internal affairs of Mexico, whether to establish or maintain a republic or to overthrow an imperial government, if Mexico chooses to accept it."

OUR GOVERNMENT WILL FINALLY RECOGNIZE THE EMPIRE.

These extracts from Mr. Seward's dispatches plainly imply two things, as the supposition that he has correctly expressed the views of the government: 1st. That from the day when the French began the siege of Puebla, the administration had determined to look on and see the life squelched out of the Mexican republic, before we would raise a finger to prevent it:—and 2d. That as soon as Maximilian's empire is firmly established, the United States will recognize it, as that manifestation of the sovereignty and independence of Mexico which her own people shall have chosen. What then becomes of the Monroe doctrine? Let it rather be asked

WHAT IS THE MONROE DOCTRINE?

Is the popular understanding of it, the correct one? Does it mean that we must maintain a republic in Mexico, when the Mexicans themselves have submitted to the establishment of an empire? Does it mean that we must force a republic upon Mexico, when the Mexicans themselves have chosen an empire?

That Mexico has a perfect right to choose her own form of government:—and that the United Stated are bound to recognize that government, whatever form it may assume, whenever it becomes firmly established, are principles that have always been regarded, recognized, and acknowledged, as among the fundamental rules of our national policy.

MUST WE ADD A GREEN ELEPHANT TO OUR MENAGERIE!

Now it is certain that such a state of things as exists in Mexico at the present time, and has been brought about by the present existing government, has never existed in Mexico at any previous period of her history. What has been the history of Mexico for the last fifty years? Has it not been a history of continual civil war and commotion? Has not that unhappy country been torn by faction, and by the quarrels of the different races by which it has been inhabited, for a period far beyond the recollection of most of my readers? Has not Mexico been dismembered because she could never establish or maintain for herself a government of sufficient stability to pay her debts? Suppose our government does demand the withdrawal of Maximilian and the demand is acceded to. Do we wish to plunge Mexico again into her former troubles and anarchy? Do we wish to see re-enacted the civil wars of Santa Anna, of Altamont, of Arista, of Comonfort, of Miramon and of Juarez? Do we wish to do over again the work that Maximilian has done so well, and that we are anxious to undo? Is not the white elephant and the black elephant that we already have on our hands quite as much menagerie as we can manage? Must we have a green elephant also? Does the Monroe doctrine require this?

TWO INTERPRETATIONS OF THE DOCTRINE.

There are two interpretations to the Monroe doctrine. According to one, we would be bound to re-establish a republican government in Mexico, even to the extent of going to war against France, and even if it should manifestly appear that the Mexican people themselves desire, and have chosen a monarchy. It is believed by those who are best informed on the subject, that there are few members of Congress who hold this to be the true interpretation of the doctrine. According to the other interpretation we are bound to leave the Mexican people to decide for themselves what form of government they prefer, and we are further bound to acquiesce in that decision. I am aware that this is a novel interpretation of the Monroe doctrine. But this is probably the interpretation which Mr. Seward puts upon it, and there is reason to believe that this view will meet with a warm support in the next Congress. If we insist upon the enforcement of the Monroe doctrine under the first interpretation, and as it has been popularly but perhaps erroneously understood, we will be obliged to give up and abandon another, equally cherished, and equally important principle of our government. That, to acknowledge and recognize the government de facto whenever such a government has been established.

OUR SETTLED POLICY TO RECOGNIZE THE GOVERNMENT DE FACTO.

This principle has been well settled, and has always been acted on by our government without deviation. Our ministers abroad have always been imperatively instructed to act upon it. The diplomatic correspondence of Daniel Webster, of Edward Everett, of Henry Clay, and of Lewis Cass, when these gentlemen were severally Secretary of State, is full of such instructions, and abounds in illustrations of this principle. The present Secretary of State has had nothing to do but to follow those illustrious precedents. And he has followed them. In the case of Mexico he has been particular in instructing our ministers abroad that the United States would not interfere with what has been going on in Mexico during the last four years, and that we would, in the end, recognize the government which should be de facto established.

On the 15th of December, 1862, after the French army had landed at Vera Cruz, but before active operations had been commenced, Mr. Seward wrote to Mr. Romero: "The United States deplore the war which has arisen between the republic of Mexico and France. They are not, however, a party to that war, and they can act in regard to it only upon principles which have always governed them heretofore, in similar cases." On the 11th of September, 1863, after the capture of the City of Mexico by the French, Mr. Seward, in a letter to our minister at Vienna, says: "The United States adopted and have maintained entire neutrality between the belligerents, in harmony with the traditional policy in regard to foreign wars." And on the 9th of October, the same year, he writes to Mr. Motley, at Vienna: "The United States practice, in regard to Mexico, in every phase of the war, the non-intervention which they require," etc. And on the 23d of October, 1863, he wrote to our Minister to England: "The United States, consistently with their principles, can do no otherwise than leave the destinies of Mexico in the keeping of her own people, and recognize their sovereignty and independence in whatever form they themselves shall choose that this sovereignty and independence shall be manifested."

No one can read these extracts from Mr. Seward's diplomatic correspondence, and compare them with what had then taken place in Mexico, without being convinced that it never was the intention of the preceding administration to save the Mexican republic from extinction; nay, without being convinced that the preceding administration had foreseen, from the first, that the Mexican republic was doomed to extinction, and had made up their minds to acquiesce in that extinction. The triple alliance of France, England and Spain, against Mexico, was concluded by a treaty signed at London, October, 31, 1861, of which our government had immediate notice. Did our government protest against this? Not at all. The allied forces landed at Vera Cruz during the succeeding winter. Still no protest. On the other hand our government acquiesced in the justice of the war made by France against Mexico, and thus bound ourselves to recognize the government which should be established by the successful belligerent.

After a careful study of Mr. Seward's diplomatic correspondence, it is impossible to doubt that he clearly foresaw that such a government as would be established in Mexico by Napoleon and Maximilian would be gratefully received and eagerly embraced by the Mexican people; and that they themselves, in the course of two or three years, would rally around it and secure its perpetuity. In his dispatch to Mr. Motley, our minister to Austria, October 9, 1863, he says: "War exists between France and Mexico. The United States has neither a right nor any disposition to intervene by force in the internal affairs of Mexico, whether to establish or to maintain a republican or even a domestic government there, or to overthrow an imperial or a foreign one, if Mexico shall choose to establish or accept it." And, in a dispatch to Mr. Dayton, our minister to France, on the 23d of October, 1863, he says: "The United States can do no otherwise than leave the destinies of Mexico in the keeping of her own people, and recognize their sovereignty and independence in whatever form they themselves shall choose that this sovereignty and independence shall be manifested." These are weighty words. Let them be carefully examined. They can bear only one interpretation, namely, that the United States has no right to force, and will not force, a republic upon Mexico, if the Mexican people desire a monarchy; and that the United States must and will recognize the present government of Mexico as soon as it shall become apparent that it is the choice of the Mexican people.

CHAPTER X.

What is the Monroe Doctrine?—Is it a Constitutional Enactment?—Is it an Irrepealable Law?—Absurdity of the Doctrine—It has no Binding Force—Why it ought to be Repudiated.

THE opposition to the Mexican empire, in the United States, arises chiefly from an impression which prevails, to the effect that the present government in Mexico has been established in contravention of the Monroe doctrine, and that it is incumbent upon the people of the United States to support that doctrine, even to the extent of destroying the government which has existed in Mexico for the last three years. The impression prevails in regard to the Monroe doctrine, that, although it is no more than the mere dictum of one man, uttered forty-three years ago, yet it constitutes a law of binding force which there is no power in the American people to repeal, which never can be repealed; which must forever remain in full force; which, although given to a former generation, must be observed by the present generation and all subsequent generations; and that this doctrine requires the United States to take Mexico under our special protection, and to force a certain form of government upon her, even when her people desire another form of government. The popular understanding of the Monroe doctrine is, that the Mexican people are to be forever debarred from the exercise of the right enjoyed by all nations, of choosing their form of government for themselves. The popular understanding of the Monroe doctrine is, that republicanism is the only form of government that Mexico can ever have, and that the United States must force the Mexicans to have that, and to have no other form of government.

What is this Monroe doctrine? Is it a part of the Constitution of the United States, which can never be amended? No: it is not a part of the Constitution. Is it an irrepealable law? Is it a law passed by Congress and signed by the President? No: it is not even a law, unless Mr. Monroe had the individual right to make laws. Was he ever empowered to make laws? laws, too, which can never be repealed?

In these latter days we have dared to lay our hands upon the Constitution; to expunge from it one article, and to alter and amend it in other respects. Is the Monroe doctrine something superior to that sacred instrument? Are we to be told that the Constitution is nothing; that it may be tinkered and patched at pleasure; but that we are to touch not the Monroe doctrine?

Let us examine, and see what this Monroe doctrine is.

In the first place, the Monroe doctrine did not

originate with Mr. Monroe. It is of British origin. It originated with the eminent British statesman, Mr. Canning. Mr. Canning first suggested the ideas to Mr. Rush, our minister to England, Mr. Rush wrote them out and sent them to John Quincy Adams, our Secretary of State, and Mr. Adams communicated them to Mr. Monroe, and prevailed upon him to introduce them into his message. Mr. Buchanan gives all the facts, as follow:

"The allied powers of Europe had triumphed over Napoleon, and had restored the elder branch of the Bourbons, in the person of Louis XVIII. to the throne of France. Emboldened by this success, Russia, Austria, and Prussia, in 1815, formed the holy alliance. To this France, and nearly all the other continental powers, soon afterward acceded. Great Britain, however, stood aloof and refused to become a party to it. The object of the allies was to abolish liberal governments on the continent of Europe, and to maintain the divine right of sovereigns to rule according to their own discretion; in short, to roll back the tide of progress toward free institutions, and to restore the old despotisms as they had existed before the French revolution. Accordingly France was deputed to destroy by force of arms, the liberal government of the Cortes in Spain, and to restore the implacable and bigoted Ferdinand VII. to absolute power. In 1823, a French army, commanded by the Duke d'Angouleme, invaded

Spain, and in a single campaign accomplished these objects.

"In the year before the date of this expedition, the government of the United States had formally acknowledged the independence of the different southern republics, formerly Spanish colonies; and an appropriation of one hundred thousand dollars had been made (May 4, 1822,) by Congress to defray the expenses of missions to these 'independent nations on the American continent.'

"Whilst the French invasion was in successful progress, the British government became satisfied that the allies, after crushing the Spanish liberals, intended to employ their arms in assisting Ferdinand VII to subjugate what they termed his rebellious colonies on this side of the Atlantic. To such an enterprise Great Britain was strenuously opposed, and she resolved to resist it If successful, this would prove to be a severe blow to her trade in that quarter of the world—an interest to which she has ever been sensitively alive.

"To avert the impending danger, Mr. Canning, then the British Minister for Foreign Affairs, in August, 1823, proposed to Mr. Rush, then the American minister in London, that the two governments should immediately unite in publishing 'a joint declaration before Europe,' manifesting their opposition to the policy and purposes of the alliance in regard to this continent. This expressed the opinion that the recovery of the colonies by Spain was hopeless; that their recognition as independent States was one of time and circumstances; that the two powers were not disposed, however to interpose obstacles in the way to any arrangements by amicable negotiations between the colonies and Spain, but that, whilst they aimed at the acquisition of no portion of these colonies for themselves, they would not see the transfer of any of them to a third power with indifference. Mr. Canning also observed that in his opinion such a joint declaration by Great Britain and the United States would alone prove sufficient to prevent the allies from any forcible interference against the former Spanish colonies. For those reasons he earnestly urged Mr. Rush to become a party to it on behalf of his government. Although Mr. Rush had no direct instructions to warrant him in such an act, and this he had communicated to Mr. Canning, yet he wisely agreed to assume the responsibility, but upon one express condition. This was that the British government should first acknowledge the independence of the American republics, as the United States had already done. Mr. Canning, though resolved on defeating the projects of alliance against the republics, was not prepared at the time to take this decisive step, and therefore the joint declaration was never made.

"Mr. Rush, in his dispatch of September 19, 1823, to Mr. John Quincy Adams, then Secretary of State, communicated to him a lucid statement of these negotiations, with explanatory documents. After these had been considered by President Monroe, he sent them, with his own views on the subject, to Mr. Jefferson, and asked his advice as to the course which ought to be pursued by the government to ward off the threatened danger.

"Mr. Jefferson's answer is dated at Monticello, on the 24th of October, 1823. It is earnest, enthusiastic, and eloquent, displaying in old age the statesmanlike sagacity and ardent patriotism of the author of the Declaration of Independence. It foreshadows and recommends the 'Monroe doctrine' to the fullest extent. From its importance we quote it entire from Randall's Life of Jefferson, vol. iii., p. 491. Mr. Jefferson says: 'The question presented by the letters you have sent me is the most momentous which has ever been offered to my contemplation since that of independence. That made us a nation; this sets our compass and points the course which we are to steer through the ocean of time opening on us, and never could we embark on it under circumstances more auspicious. Our first fundamental maxim should be, never to entangle ourselves in the broils of Europe. Our second, *never to suffer Europe to meddle with cis-Atlantic affairs.* America, North and South, has a set of interests distinct from those of Europe, and peculiarly her own. She should, therefore, have a system of her own, separate and apart from that of Europe. While the last is laboring to become the domicil of despotism, our endeavor should surely be to make our hemisphere that of freedom. One nation, most of all, could disturb us in this pursuit; she now offers to lead, aid, and accompany us in it. By acceding to our proposition we detach her from the bands of despots, bring her mighty weight into the scale of free government, and emancipate a continent at one stroke, which might otherwise linger long in doubt and difficulty. Great Britain is the nation which can do us the most harm of any one, or all on earth; and with her on our side, we need not fear the whole world. With her, then, we should most seriously cherish a cordial friendship, and nothing would tend more to unite our affections than to be fighting once more side by side in the same cause. Not that I would purchase even her amity at the price of taking part in her wars. But the war in which the present proposition might engage us, should that be its consequence, is not her war, but ours. Its object is to introduce and establish the American system of keeping out of our land all foreign powers, of never permitting those of Europe to intermeddle with the affairs of our nations. It is to maintain our own principle, not to depart from it; and if, to facilitate this, we can effect a division in the body of the European powers, and draw over to our side its most powerful member, surely we should do it. But I am clearly of Mr. Canning's opinion, that it will prevent instead of provoke war. With Great Britain withdrawn from their scale and shifted into that of our two continents, all Europe combined would not undertake such a war. For how would they propose to get at either enemy without superior fleets? Nor is the occasion to be slighted which this proposition offers of declaring our protest against the atrocious violations of the rights of nations by the interference of any one in the internal affairs of another so flagitiously begun by Bonaparte, and now continued by the equally lawless alliance calling itself holy.

"'But we have first to ask ourselves a question: Do we wish to acquire to our own confederacy any one or more of the Spanish provinces? I candidly confess that I have ever looked on Cuba as the most interesting addition that could ever be made to our system of States. The control which, with Florida Point, this island would give us over the Gulf of Mexico, and the countries and isthmus bordering thereon, would fill up the measure of our political well-being. Yet as I am sensible that this can never be obtained, even with her own consent, but by war, and its independence, which is our second interest (and especially its independence of England), can be secured without it, I have no hesitation in abandoning my first wish to future chances, and accepting its independence, with peace and the friendship of England, rather than its association at the expense of war and her enmity.

"'I could honestly, therefore, join in the declaration proposed: that we aim not at the acquisition of any of those possessions; that we will not stand in the way of any amicable arrangement between them and the mother country; but that we will oppose, with all our means, the forcible interposition of any other power as auxiliary, stipendiary, or under any pretext, and most especially their transfer to any other power by conquest, cession, or acquisition in any other way. I should think it advisable, therefore, that the Executive should encourage the British government to a continuance in the dispositions expressed in these letters, by an assurance of his concurrence with them as far as his authority goes; and that, as it may lead to war, the declaration of which requires an act of Congress, the case shall be laid before them for consideration, at their first meeting, and under the reasonable aspect in which it is seen by himself.

"'I have been so long weaned from political subjects, and have so long ceased to take any interest in them, that I am sensible I am not qualified to offer opinions on them worthy of any attention. But the question now proposed involves consequences so lasting, and effects so decisive of our future destinies, as to rekindle all the interest I have heretofore felt on such occasions, and to induce me to the hazard of opinions which will prove only my wish to contribute still my mite toward any thing which may be useful to our country. And, praying you to accept it only at what it is worth, I add the assurance of my constant and affectionate friendship and respect.'

"President Monroe, thus fortified by the support of Mr. Jefferson, proceeded to announce in his seventh annual message to Congress, of December 2, 1823, the now celebrated 'Monroe doctrine.' This summed up in his assertion, 'as a principle in which the rights and interests of the United States are involved, that the two American continents, by the free and independent condition they have assumed and maintained, are henceforth not to be considered as subjects for future colonization by any European powers.'"

It is from the above modest dimension that the Monroe doctrine of the present day has grown, and it may safely be said that Monroe himself would fail to recognize his offspring in its gigantic proportions of to-day. Mr. Monroe speaks of certain independent governments. He says that no European power must oppress them, nor control their destiny in any other manner. He says that the two American continents are henceforth not to be considered as subjects for future colonization by any European power. He does not say that we will go to war to vindicate this doctrine. But he merely says that a violation of these principles will be regarded as the manifestation of an unfriendly spirit toward us.

That is all.

HAS MAXIMILIAN VIOLATED THE MONROE DOCTRINE?

Now apply these principles to Mexico. Have they been violated by Napoleon and Maximilian? Are the Mexicans "oppressed" by the imperial government; or, on the other hand, have they been delivered from oppression?

In the second place, it is evident that the Monroe doctrine was put forth with reference to a certain state of things existing at that time, and chiefly because the English government desired it. The commercial supremacy of England was threatened with a certain danger. The interests of England and those of the United States happened to be identical at the time, and Mr. Canning had no difficulty in persuading our government to take the ground that he desired, and which ground, taken by us, would and did avert from England the threatened danger. The idea running through the whole of Mr. Jefferson's letter is plainly seen to be, a virtual alliance with England, in order to break up certain designs of some of the other European nations. Mr. Jefferson says we must never suffer Europe to meddle with cis-Atlantic affairs. Mr. Monroe does not go so far as that. Indeed, that doctrine would carry us far beyond our strength, great as that is. If "Europe" once made up its mind to meddle with the affairs of any nation in America except ours, we should be compelled either to permit such interference, or else to risk our own nationality in a war with the great European powers.

How absurd it is in the American people to fancy that Mr. Monroe could make a "doctrine" which should constitute an irrepealable law to all future generations! Suppose Mr. Monroe had enunciated certain dogmas about commerce or about finance, sound at that time, but which the experience of forty years has proved erroneous, would we be foolish enough to adhere to such financial or commercial errors now, merely because they had been doctrines of Mr. Monroe? Most certainly not. Would we not have the right to repudiate them now?

Suppose we should change the form of our own government, and choose a monarchy? The event is not impossible. All the republics that ever existed in the world, the republics of Greece, the republics of Rome, and the republics of modern times, have all fallen, and each one has been succeeded by a monarchy. What reason have we to suppose that our republic will prove an exception? The decline of constitutional liberty in America has already commenced. Commenced! did I say? It commenced in 1848 and 1850, when the Northern States refused to perform their constitutional obligations toward the South: and it has been progressing with frightful velocity during the last six years. What kind of republican government is enjoyed in Maryland and Missouri, where two thirds of the citizens are disfranchised, and those the oldest and most respected citizens of those States? What kind of a republican government is that in Missouri, where, until the 14th day of January, 1867, a clergyman could not preach nor perform any of the holy offices of religion, without first taking an iron-clad test-oath—an oath repugnant to the conscience of every christian, and which the Supreme Court of the United States has pronounced to be entirely illegal and unconstitutional? What kind of republican government is that enjoyed by the ten Southern States, with their representatives excluded from Congress, and with every prospect of negro suffrage being forced upon them?

Would it not be well for us to settle among ourselves what republican government is, before we insist upon forcing it upon the Mexicans who detest it in any form? Mr. Thaddeus Stevens says, in his place in the House of Representatives, that Pennsylvania is not a republic, and never has been. Mr. Thaddeus Stevens proclaims that the United States has not now, and never has had, a republican form of government. We are to force upon Mexico therefore, not the kind of a government that we have enjoyed during the whole period of our national existence, and under which we became, until 1860, such a prosperous, happy, and powerful nation, but some other kind of a government, which the radical politicians now in power, fancy to be a republic. According to Thaddeus Stevens and Charles Sumner, a republic is a government where thirty-six States are governed by twenty-five, and where the twenty-five force upon the other eleven institutions which are repugnant to them.

The Hon. Mr. Doolittle, Senator of the United States, in a speech, recently delivered at Philadelphia, said:—

"Our fathers in the Declaration of Independence, you remember, declared, 'we will hold the people of Great Britain as we do the rest of mankind, enemies in war, in peace friends.' Fellow-citizens, is it the best way to make peace to say to these ten States, with six or eight millions of people, covering a country as large as England and France and Italy and Germany all put together: 'You shall have no representatives in Congress; you shall have taxation without representation; we will tax you by millions; we will govern you by the representatives of the twenty-six other States; you shall have no voice in the government that taxes and governs you?' Is that the way to make peace? Fellow-citizens, I say most solemnly we have never given to that people any just cause for revolution or rebellion against the government of the United States; but if we continue to do as this majority in Congress has during the last year, deny to that people the right of representation, tax them without representation, govern them, and give them no voice in the government we shall give to them the same cause for rebellion and revolution which our fathers had for rebelling against Great Britain. I ask you, fellow-citizens, is that the way to make peace? Is that the way to restore fraternity? Is that the way to re-establish the Union? God forbid."

But if Mr. Monroe had a "doctrine," Mr. Jefferson had one too. Mr. Jefferson's doctrine was, that each one of the States is sovereign, and that a State has a right to secede from the Union. If Mr. Monroe's doctrine is sound, and of binding force, why not that of Mr. Jefferson's?

CHAPTER XI.

Policy of the Emperor Napoleon toward Mexico—Objects of the French Expedition—The Emperor Never Intended the French Troops to Remain Long in Mexico—The Arrangements for the Withdrawal of the French Troops were not made until the Stability of the Empire was Secured—Detailed Exposition, by the French Government, of the Objects and Purposes of the Emperor Napoleon—Principles upon which the Mexican Empire was Established—Why it is Supported by Napoleon—The Negotiations between France and the United States for the Withdrawal of the French Troops—France Desires a Guarantee of Neutrality on the Part of the United States—Mr. Seward Gives the Guarantee of Neutrality.

It has been made an objection to the Mexican empire, that it was not only established by a French army, but that it was the intention of the Emperor to keep it supported by a French army. I have already shown that the empire was established by the Mexican people themselves. I shall now produce some facts which will show the groundlessness of the latter objection. I shall prove that the Emperor Napoleon always intended that the French expedition should be brought to as speedy a termination as possible, and that the French troops should return to France as soon as they had afforded to the Mexican people the necessary aid to enable them to establish their government. In his instructions to General Bazaine, August

17, 1863, he says: "The reorganization of the Mexican army is one of the most important questions which should occupy your attention and that of the provisional government. It is the duty of the Minister of War to transmit special instructions to you on this point. I will confine myself to saying that the desire of the French government being to restrict, as promptly as circumstances will permit, the extent and duration of our occupation, it is essential that this reorganization should be pushed forward with all possible activity."

On the 17th of August 1865, the French government wrote to the Marquis de Montholon, French Minister at Washington, "We have already withdrawn some of our troops from Mexico, and we shall recall them all gradually, according to the re-establishment of order and the pacification of the country. We look forward with the sincerest wishes to the day when the last French soldier shall quit Mexico."

On the 18th of October, 1865, the French government wrote as follows to the Marquis de Montholon:—

"MONSIEUR DROUYN DE LHUYS TO THE MARQUIS DE MONTHOLON.—(Confidential.)

"[Translation.]

"MINISTRE DES AFFAIRES ETRANGERES,

"PARIS, *October* 18, 1865.

"MONSIEUR LE MARQUIS:—I have taken several occasions since two months to advise you of the dispositions of the Imperial government concerning the duration of the occupation of Mexico by the French troops. I told you, in my despatch of August 17, that we called with our most sincere wishes for the day when the last French soldier should leave the country and that the Cabinet of Washington could contribute to hasten that moment. On the 2d of September I renewed to you the assurance of our strong desire to withdraw our auxiliary corps so soon as circumstances should allow it."

On the 10th of January, 1866, M. Drouyn de Lhuys, the French Secretary of State for Foreign Affairs, handed to Mr. Bigelow a memorandum in writing, which says:

" [Translation.—Memorandum.]

" The Washington Cabinet recognizes the right which we have, like any sovereign nation, to make war on Mexico. On our side we desire to observe the principle of non-intervention. Does not the approximating of these two points offer the basis of a common understanding?

" To make war is not only to overthrow fortifications and kill a certain number of men, it is especially to assure a right infringed upon, the vindication of which has rendered necessary the employment of arms. Until this end is fully attained, the means of execution incident to war remain legitimate. In Mexico we hope to obtain before long the guarantees which we have sought and which are to complete our final arrangements with the Emperor Maximilian. At that moment the mission of our troops will be accomplished, and they can return to France."

The public mind in the United States has been confused and perplexed in regard to the Mexican question, and has been led to form wrong conclusions as to what national honor and our national interests require of us, in regard to its settlement. The idea has been put prominently forward, that the Emperor Napoleon regrets what he has done in Mexico; that it was a great mistake on his part; that he is anxious to wash his hands of the whole affair; and that he withdraws the French troops from Mexico in order to leave Maximilian to his fate, and because he believes that the empire in Mexico cannot stand without French bayonets: a support which he finds to be too costly for him longer to afford. This idea is radically erroneous.

OBJECTS OF THE FRENCH EXPEDITION.

Napoleon organized the expedition to Mexico with certain objects in view. These objects were, in brief, first, to deliver the Mexican people from that condition of anarchy and helplessness under which they had groaned for forty years, deluded by the name of a republic, but which was a republic only in name; second, to offer to the Mexican nation a government whose stability should be guaranteed by the great powers of Europe, and which should secure to the Mexican people as perfect and the same liberty that is enjoyed by the people of England, France, or any other well regulated, constitutional monarchy, and all the other blessings of a good and stable government; third, to inaugurate and set on foot measures for the development of the vast and inexhaustible mineral resources and agricultural wealth of Mexico; fourth, to give to Mexico those facilities for transportation, in the shape of railroads, which would enable her to enjoy her full share of the great carrying trade between Europe and the East Indies.

THESE OBJECTS HAVE BEEN FULLY ACCOMPLISHED.

These objects are now regarded by Napoleon as having been accomplished. The government which Napoleon offered to the Mexican people was accepted by them, first by the Assembly of Notables, and afterward by the cheerful acquiescence of four fifths of the Mexican people. No one who is well informed on Mexican affairs disputes this, nor can it be denied that four fifths of the Mexican people are ardently attached to Maximilian's government, and sincerely desire its continuance. The stability and perpetuity of this government is beside guaranteed by the stipulations of a treaty between France, Austria, Belgium and Maximilian.

The Emperor Napoleon therefore, can not only look with pride upon his work, but he can leave it, and withdraw the French troops, with the full knowledge that the Mexican people themselves will sustain the empire, the government of their own choice. In establishing this government, Napoleon was no doubt moved by a laudable and honorable ambition. Having established it, therefore, upon a firm and durable basis, his first care was to secure its permanence and stability. He knew that it would be vain to look for its recognition by the United States, until its ability to sustain itself had been demonstrated. He took pains to provide the Emperor Maximilian, therefore, with able and experienced officers for every department of his government, civil as well as military; and, second, to make such treaties with the great powers of Europe as should secure the end he had in view. By the means alluded to under the first head, the internal administration of affairs in Mexico for the last two years, has been such as to make that country prosperous and its people happy and contented, a condition which Mexico has not enjoyed before for forty years past. Its finances although not in a perfectly satisfactory condition, are in a far better state than ever before; trade and commerce are flourishing to an extraordinary degree and are rapidly increasing; the revenues of the country are steadily increasing; the people are actively engaged in all the avocations of industry; and the vast agricultural and mineral resources of Mexico are being developed to an extent never before dreamed of. Satisfactory progress has been made in the construction of the great railroad from Vera Cruz to the capital; schools and academies are in successful operation, and the Mexico of to-day is far more like the United States than the Mexico of five years ago.

HOW THESE OBJECTS WERE ACCOMPLISHED.

This state of things has been brought about mainly by the active exertions of the officers, civil and military, who have been supplied by the French Government, acting under the immediate and personal supervision of Maximilian and the Empress Carlotta.

These are the facts to which the Emperor Napoleon could point, if the United States, not satisfied with the withdrawal of the French troops, were to request him to withdraw from Maximilian the moral support of the French government also. He could say in substance to Mr. Seward:—"Excuse me, sir, if I decline your polite invitation. My movements in Mexico were conducted with great deliberation, and in the sight of the whole world. I waited a whole year, to see if you would interpose in behalf of your Monroe doctrine. Instead of doing so, you said that you did not see a struggling, dying republic in Mexico, but that you saw there two belligerent parties, and that you would look on, and see us fight it out on that line. Well, sir, we have done so. I found Mexico torn with civil commotions, a prey to faction, and deeply in debt to the citizens of France. You had refused to help her to maintain a republican government. I have given her a government which holds out the prospect of stability. Under the government of Maximilian, Mexico can now become a happy and prosperous nation."

The whole history of the Emperor of France, and a careful study of his character, shows him to be a man of remarkable foresight and sagacity; a man who never undertook any enterprise hastily; a man who has seldom or never failed in any public enterprise that he has once embraced. He is irrevocably committed, to support the empire in Mexico. If he regards the establishment of a good government in that country, and the deliverance of the Mexican nation from its former condition of anarchy and weakness, as one of the greatest acts of his reign, and as one of the greatest achievements of modern times, what candid and intelligent person will deny that it is so? Will not history so record it?

If it be asked, "Why then, does Napoleon withdraw his troops from Mexico?" this is the answer: because they are no longer needed there. The object for which they were sent there, has been fully accomplished. They have remained in Mexico until the government of the empire is firmly established, and until their presence is no longer required to give stability to that government. When the last squadron of those troops shall have embarked at Vera Cruz, they will leave behind them an army of forty thousand native Mexican troops, and French and Austrian volunteers, all veteran soldiers, well armed, admirably disciplined, and commanded by French and Austrian officers. The arrangements for the substitution of this Mexican army for the French troops, have been quietly made by the Emperor Maximilian, during the whole of the year 1866.

Agreement between the United States and France.

But it may be well to remember that certain negotiations between our government and that of France preceded the announcement by Napoleon of his intention to withdraw the French troops. In the first place, Napoleon sought to know whether, in case those troops were withdrawn, the United States would continue to maintain their policy of neutrality and non-intervention toward Mexico? On the 12th of February, 1866, Mr. Seward gives a plain and direct answer to this question. In his dispatch of that date to the Marquis de Montholon, he assures the French government that, in case the French troops are withdrawn from Mexico, the United States will continue to maintain our policy of neutrality and non-intervention toward Mexico. This was all that Napoleon desired, for he immediately rejoined, that that assurance was perfectly satisfactory to him; and on the 5th of April, 1866, M. Drouyn de Lhuys wrote to the French minister here, and desired him to convey to the United States government the information that, depending upon that pledge of neutrality upon our part, the French troops would be withdrawn from Mexico in detachments. Substantially, therefore, the withdrawal of the French troops from Mexico is to take place in pursuance of a solemn agreement between France and the United States, by which we are bound, by every principle of honor, to continue to maintain our policy of neutrality toward Mexico.

But the policy of the Emperor Napoleon may be found clearly set forth in his own language, and in the State papers of the French foreign office. His instructions to General Forey, of July 3, 1862, and to General Bazaine, August 17, 1863, are worthy of the most careful attention of the reader. They will be found on pages 37 and 49.

On the 9th of January, 1866, the French government wrote to the French minister at Washington, as follow:

"THE MINISTER OF FOREIGN AFFAIRS TO THE FRENCH MINISTER AT WASHINGTON.

"PARIS, *9th of January*, 1866.

"M. LE MARQUIS:—I had desired you, by the Emperor's order, to make known to the cabinet of Washington the views of his majesty's government upon the affairs of Mexico, and conformably to my instructions you have brought to Mr. Seward's knowledge the dispatch I had the honor to forward you on the 18th of October. The Secretary of State replied to that dispatch by a communication he was good enough to address to you on the 6th of December, of which I think it advisable to recapitulate here the principal points.

"According to Mr. Seward, the presence of a foreign force in a country adjacent to the Union cannot but be a cause of uneasiness and disquiet. This state of things entails upon the Federal governnment inconvenient expenses, and may bring about collisions. The chief reason for the displeasure of the United States, however, is not the fact of there being a foreign army in Mexico, still less that the army is French. The cabinet of Washington recognizes the right of every sovereign nation to make war, provided the exercise of that right does not threaten the security and legitimate influence of the Union. But the French army has gone to Mexico to overthrow a national republican government, and with the avowed object of establishing upon the ruins a foreign monarchical government. Mr. Seward sets forth in this respect how much the people of the United States are attached to the institutions they have adopted, and repudiating all ideas of propagandism in favor of those institutions, he claims for the various peoples of the New World, the right of securing to themselves this form of government according to their convenience. He would consider it inadmissible that European powers should intervene in those countries with the idea of destroying the republican form to substitute kingdoms and empires in its stead.

"'Having thus frankly defined our position,' adds Mr. Seward, 'I submit the question to the judgment of France, while sincerely wishing that great nation may find it compatible with its true interests and its high honor to abandon the aggressive attitude it has taken up in Mexico.'

"In concluding, Mr. Seward recalls, as a reason for his hope of arriving at a happy solution, the ancient affection of the United States for France, and the value every American citizen has always attached to our friendship in past times, and continues to attach to it in future.

"I have not failed to submit this communication to the Emperor, and after having maturely examined the considerations laid down by Mr. Seward, his majesty's government remains convinced that the divergence of views between the two cabinets is, above all, the result of an erroneous appreciation of our intentions.

"Our expedition, I need hardly say, was not intended as hostile to the peoples of the New World, and assuredly still less to those of the Union. France cannot forget that she has contributed to establish them with her blood, and among the number of glorious recollections the old monarchy bequeathed to us, there was not one of which Napoleon I. was prouder, and which

Napoleon III. is less disposed to repudiate. If, on the other hand, we had been actuated by an idea of ill-will toward that republic, would we have endeavored from the beginning to obtain the assistance of the Federal government, which, like ourselves, had claims to advance? Would we have observed neutrality in the great crisis the United States have passed through? And now would we be disposed, as we declare with the greatest frankness, to hasten as much as may be possible the time of recalling our troops?

"Our only object has been to claim the satisfaction to which we had a right, by resorting to coercive measures after having exhausted all others. It is known how numerous and legitimate were the demands of French subjects. We took up arms in presence of a series of flagrant injuries, and striking denials of justice. The complaints of the United States were certainly less numerous and less important, when they too were induced, some years ago, to employ force against Mexico.

"The French army did not bring monarchical traditions upon Mexican soil in the folds of its flag. The cabinet of Washington is not unaware that there have been for a certain number of years a considerable group of men in that country who, despairing of finding order under the conditions of the system then existing, cherished the idea of returning to monarchy. Their opinions had been shared by one of the late Presidents of that republic, who had even offered to use his power to favor the establishment of royalty. Seeing the degree of anarchy to which the government of Juarez had fallen, they thought the time had come to appeal to the sentiment of the nation, tired, like themselves, of the state of dissolution in which its resources were exhausted. We did not think we ought to discourage this last effort of a powerful party, whose origin is of prior date to our expedition; but, faithful to the maxims of public right we hold in common with the United States, we declared that this question must be referred solely to the suffrages of the Mexican people.

"The idea of the Emperor's government was defined by his majesty himself, in a letter addressed to the commander-in-chief of our army after the capture of Puebla. 'Our object, you are aware,' said the Emperor, 'is not to impose upon the Mexicans a government contrary to their wishes, nor to make our successes subserve the triumph of any party. I desire that Mexico should be born into new life, and that, speedily regenerated by a government based upon the national will, upon the principles of order and progress, upon respect for the law of nations, she may recognize, by friendly relations, that she owes to France her repose and her prosperity.'

"The Mexican people uttered its decision. The Emperor Maximilian was summoned by the wish of the country. This government appeared to us of a nature to bring about peace at home, and good faith in international relations. We granted it our support.

"We went, therefore, to Mexico to carry out the right of war which Mr. Seward fully admits that we possess, and not by virtue of a principle of intervention, upon which we profess the same doctrine as the United States. We went there, not to make proselytes to monarchy, but to obtain reparation and guarantees we were entitled to claim, and we support the government founded with the assent of the population, because we expect from it the satisfaction of our complaints with indispensable securities for the future.

"As we seek neither an exclusive interest nor the realization of an ambitious idea, our sincerest wish is to hasten as much as possible the time when we shall be able with security to our fellow-subjects and dignity to ourselves, to recall what remains in that country of the *corps d'armee* we sent there. As I informed you in the dispatch to which Mr. Seward's communcation replies, it depends greatly upon the Federal government to facilitate, in this respect, the accomplishment of its desire. The doctrine of the United States, resting, like our own, upon the principle of the national will, is not incompatible with the existence of monarchical institutions; and President Johnson in his message, like Mr. Seward, in his dispatch, repudiates all idea of propagandism, even upon the American continent, in favor of republican institutions. The cabinet of Washington entertains friendly relations with the court of the Brazils, and it did not refuse to enter into relations with the Mexican empire, in 1822. No fundamental maxim, no precedent of the diplomatic history of the Union, therefore, creates a necessary antagonism between the United States, and the system which, in Mexico, has replaced a power which has, continually and systematically violated its most positive obligations toward other nations.

"Mr. Seward seems to make the government of the Emperor Maximilian a two-fold reproach as to the difficulties it meets with and the aid it borrows from foreign forces But the resistance against which it has found itself compelled to struggle has no particular reference to the form of its institutions. It suffers the ordinary fate of new authorities, and its chief misfortune is to have to endure the consequences of the disorders which have arisen under previous governments. Which of those governments, in fact, has not found armed competitors and has enjoyed undisputed authority in peace? Revolts and intestine wars were then the normal state of the country, and the opposition raised by some military chiefs to the establishment of the empire is only the natural consequence of the habits of want of discipline and anarchy, of which the authorities to which it succeeds have been the victims.

"As for the support the Mexican government receives from our army, and which Belgian and Austrian volunteers give it also, no attack is thereby made upon the independence of its resolutions or upon the perfect liberty of its acts. What State is there which has not had need of allies, either to constitute or to defend it? And have not great powers, like France and England, for instance, almost constantly maintained foreign troops in their armies? *When the United States fought for their emancipation, did the assistance given by France to their efforts prevent that great popular movement from being truly national? Will any one say that the struggle against the South was not equally a national war because thousands of Irish and Germans fought under the Union flag?* It would be impossible, therefore, to dispute the character of the Mexican government, and to consider as a motive of dislike toward it either the resistance it must conquer to consolidate itself, or the foreign troops who will have aided it to cause security and order to revive in a country so long and so deeply agitated."

"Such an undertaking is assuredly worthy of being appreciated by a nation so enlightened as the United States, especially calculated to reap advantage from it. In place of a country incessantly troubled, which has given them so many subjects of complaint, and upon which they themselves have even been obliged to make war, they would find a pacified country, henceforth offering guarantees of security and vast outlets to their commerce. Far from injuring their rights or impairing their influence, it is they in especial who ought to profit by the work of reorganization being carried out in Mexico.

"To sum up, M. le Marquis, *the United States recognize the right we had to make war in Mexico; upon the other hand, like them, we admit the principle of non-intervention. This two-fold admission seems to me to offer the elements of an agreement.* The right of making war, which belongs, as Mr. Seward states, to every sovereign nation, implies the right of securing the results of war. We have not crossed the ocean solely with the intention of displaying our power and of inflicting chastisement upon the Mexican government.

"After a series of useless reclamations, we must demand guarantees against the return of the violence from which our fellow-subjects have suffered so cruelly, and we cannot expect these guarantees from a government whose bad faith we had so often experienced. We find them now in the establishment of a regular power, which shows itself disposed honestly to keep its engagements. Under these circumstances we hope that the legitimate object of our expedition will soon be attained, *and we are hastening to make arrangements with the Emperor Maximilian which, while satisfying our interests and our dignity, allow us to consider the part of our army upon Mexican soil at an end. The Emperor has ordered me to write in this sense to his minister in Mexico.*

"We return after that period to the principle of non-intervention, and from the moment we accept it as our rule of conduct, our interest and honor require us to demand its equal application by all. Relying upon the equitable spirit of the Washington cabinet, we expect from it the assurance that the American people will conform to the law they invoke by maintaining a strict neutrality with regard to Mexico. When you shall have informed me of the resolution of the American government in this matter, I shall be in a position to acquaint you with the result of our negotiation with the Emperor Maximilian for the return of our troops.

"I request you to hand Mr. Seward a copy of this dispatch, in reply to his communication of the 6th of December last, asking him to bring it to the knowledge of President Johnson; and I rest with confidence for the examination of the arguments it contains upon the traditional sentiments recalled by the note of the Secretary of State of the Union.

"DROUYN DE LHUYS."

This admirable state paper needs no comment, for it is its own commentary. But every line, and every word of it is worthy of the most attentive consideration. No one, who has not read this dispatch, can fully comprehend the Mexican question; and no one who has given it an attentive perusal, can be misled upon any vital point concerning that question. In our intercourse with France, on this subject, we must be guided by, and conform to, the principles of international law. None of those principles are more clearly settled than that which declares that the right to make war implies and carries with it the right to secure the results of war. Napoleon did not cross the Atlantic to punish the Mexican people. He came to Mexico to secure guarantees for the claims which France had against Mexico, and these guarantees he could not expect to find in a government whose perfidy even the United States had proved. He found those guarantees, finally, in the establishment of the present government; a government founded, as he claims, upon the will of the Mexican people themselves. He went to Mexico to obtain these guarantees. Having thus obtained them, "we sustain the government," says M. Drouyn de Lhuys, "which is founded on the consent of the people, because we expect from it the satisfaction of our wrongs." And he then informs Mr. Seward that as soon as the latter will assure him that the United States will maintain neutrality toward Mexico, arrangements can be made for the return of the French troops to France, because they will have accomplished the objects of the Mexican expedition.

APPENDIX.

I.

"TREATY BETWEEN THE EMPEROR OF FRANCE, AND THE EMPEROR OF MEXICO.

"THE government of the Emperor of the French and that of the Emperor of Mexico, animated with an equal desire to secure the re-establishment of order in Mexico, and to consolidate the new empire, have resolved to regulate by a convention the conditions of the stay of the French troops in that country, and have named their plenipotentiaries to that effect, viz.:

"The Emperor of the French, M. Charles Herbet, minister plenipotentiary of the first class, councillor of state, director of the ministry of foreign affairs, grand officer of the Legion of Honor, etc.; and the Emperor of Mexico, M. Joaquin Velasquez de Leon, his minister of state without portfolio, grand officer of the distinguished order of Our Lady of Guadaloupe, etc.; who, after having communicated to each other their full powers, agreed on the following provisions:

"ARTICLE 1. The French troops at present in Mexico shall be reduced as soon as possible to a corps of twenty thousand men, including the foreign legion. This corps, in order to safeguard the interests which led to the intervention, shall remain temporarily in Mexico on the conditions laid down by the following articles.

"ARTICLE 2. The French troops shall evacuate Mexico in proportion as the Emperor of Mexico shall be able to organize the troops necessary to replace them.

"ARTICLE 3. The foreign legion in the service of France, composed of eight thousand men, shall, nevertheless, remain in Mexico six years after all the other French troops shall have been recalled in conformity with Article 2. From that moment the said legion shall pass into the service and pay of the Mexican government, which reserves to itself the right of abridging the duration of the employment of the foreign legion in Mexico.

"ARTICLE 4. The points of the territory to be occupied by the French troops, as well as the military expeditions of the said troops, if there be any, shall be determined in common accord, directly between the Emperor of Mexico and the commandant-in-chief of the French corps.

"ARTICLE 5. On all the points where the garrison shall not be exclusively composed of Mexican troops, the military command shall devolve on the French commander. In case of expeditions combined of French and Mexican troops, the superior direction of those troops shall also belong to the French commander.

"ARTICLE 6. The French commanders shall not interfere with any branch of the Mexican administration.

"ARTICLE 7. So long as the requirements of the French corps d'armee shall necessitate a two monthly service of transports between France and Vera Cruz, the expense of the said service, fixed at the sum of four hundred thousand francs per voyage, (going and returning,) shall be paid by Mexico.

"ARTICLE 8. The naval stations which France maintains in the West Indies and in the Pacific Ocean shall often send vessels to show the French flag in the ports of Mexico.

"ARTICLE 9. The expenses of the French expedition to Mexico, to be paid by the Mexican government, are fixed at the sum of two hundred and seventy million francs for the whole duration of the expedition down to the 1st of July, 1864. That sum shall bear interest at the rate of three per cent. per annum. From the 1st of July all the expense of the Mexican army shall be at the charge of Mexico.

"ARTICLE 10. The indemnity to be paid to France by the Mexican government for the pay and maintenance of the troops of the corps d'armee after the 1st of July, 1864, remains fixed at the sum of one thousand francs a year for each man.

"ARTICLE 11. The Mexican government shall hand over to the French government the sum of sixty-six million francs in bonds of the loan at the rate of issue, viz.: fifty-four million francs, to be deducted from the debt mentioned in Article 9, and twelve million francs as an instalment of the indemnities due to Frenchmen in virtue of Article 14 of the present convention.

"ARTICLE 12. For the payment of the surplus of the war expenses, and for acquitting the charges in Articles 7, 10, and 14, the Mexican government engages to pay annually to France the sum of twenty-five millions in specie. That sum shall be imputed, first, to the sums due in virtue of articles 7 and 10; and secondly, to the amount, interest and principal, of the sum fixed in Article 9; thirdly, to the indemnities which shall remain due to the French subjects in virtue of Article 14 and following.

"ARTICLE 13. The Mexican government shall pay, on the last day of every month, into the hands of the paymaster-general of the army, what shall be due for covering the expenses of the French troops remaining in Mexico, in conformity with Article 10.

"ARTICLE 14. The Mexican government engages to indemnify French subjects for the wrongs they have newly suffered, and which were the original cause of the expedition.

"ARTICLE 15. A mixed commission, composed of three Frenchmen and three Mexicans, appointed by their respective governments, shall meet at Mexico within three months, to examine and determine these claims.

"ARTICLE 16. A commission of revision, composed of two Frenchmen and two Mexicans, appointed in the same manner, sitting at Paris, shall proceed to the definite liquidation of the claims already admitted by the commission designated in the preceding Article, and shall decide on those which have been received for its decision.

"ARTICLE 17. The French government shall set at liberty all the Mexican prisoners of war as soon as the Emperor of Mexico shall have entered his States.

"ARTICLE 18. The present convention shall be ratified and the ratifications exchanged as early as possible.

"Done at the castle of Miramar, this 10th day of April, 1864.

"HERBET
"JOAQUIN VELASQUEZ DE LEON."

II.

"THE MINISTER OF FOREIGN AFFAIRS TO THE FRENCH MINISTER IN WASHINGTON.

"PARIS, 17*th of August*, 1865.

"MONSIEUR LE MARQUIS:—The minister of the United States addressed to me on the 1st instant the note of which you will find a copy annexed. In the answer, of which a copy is also given, which I sent by the Emperor's command to this communication, I felt bound to declare to Mr. Bigelow that, always ready to reply to demands for explanations addressed to us in a friendly manner, *we could not think of responding to interpellations expressed in a threatening tone relative to vague allegations founded on equivocal documents.* At the same time I took the opportunity afforded by the communication of the minister of the United States, to remind him that, as observers of a scrupulous neutrality in all the internal questions which may agitate or divide the American Union, we were entitled to rely on the exact and loyal reciprocity promised to us on his part with regard to the affairs of Mexico. We do rely on it, in fact, and yet we are unable to conceal from ourselves that there is some difficulty in conciliating certain recent facts and manifestations, of which we cannot mistake the character, with the assurances we have received.

"We know that our expedition, its consequences, the establishment of a monarchy in Mexico, have been viewed with displeasure in the United States; we have been told this, and we regret it. But a displeasure does not constitute a grievance, a sentiment does not create a right; and the peace of the world would be exposed to continual dangers if each State, in its relations with its neighbors, were to conduct itself solely to suit its own conveniences or preferences. In a free country, *par excellence*, like the United States, it should be known that the liberty and the right of each—State or individual—have for limits the liberty and right of others.

"*I have not here to justify our expedition to Mexico.* Obliged to do ourselves justice, we went to Mexico to seek the satisfaction which had been obstinately refused us. *We yielded to a necesssity of the same nature as that which had, at another epoch, conducted the American arms to the capital of Mexico. The Union exer-*

cised the rights of victory in all their plentitude by annexing a new State. France does not go so far; we shall leave Mexico without acquiring an inch of soil, and without reserving to ourselves any advantage not common to all other powers. After our formal declarations on this subject, and the categorical denials we have opposed to all contrary allegations, we are dispensed from replying to the persistent rumors of territorial cessions, by means of which endeavors are made to keep up irritation against us in the United States. The semblance of a government against which we made war disappeared at our approach, Far from pretending to dispose of the country, we invited and encouraged it to dispose of itself.

"In a communication which Mr. Bigelow did me the honor to address to me on the 12th of June last, he was pleased to acknowledge that the success of republican institutions in Spanish America had not been such as to encourage the United States to attempt propagating them otherwise than by example, and that, *in fine, any government which should be acceptable to the Mexicans would satisfy the United States.* There is no reason to be astonished, therefore, that Mexico, enlightened by disastrous experience, should endeavor, under a system better adapted to its instincts, to escape from the anarchical chaos into which it had been plunged by an interminable series of revolutions.

"A movement took place in the sense of monarchical ideas in favor of a liberal prince, belonging to a dynasty certainly illustrious among all, but attached to us by no bond, and with which we had just been at war. The Archduke Maximilian, called by the suffrages of the country, and proclaimed Emperor, now exercises the sovereign rights conferred on him by the Mexican nation. No other constituted power exists on Mexican soil. An ex-President, flying from village to village, is no more a head of a government than a few bands of guerillas, pillaging and infesting the high roads, are armies. Can the cabinet of Washington be ignorant of that state of things? It has itself, during four years, contested the character of a regular power to the government residing at Richmond. Are we not allowed to ask by what signs it recognizes in the person of M. Juarez the attributes of sovereignty?

"Our right, resulting from injury done to our interests, took us to Mexico. We are unwilling to leave anarchy behind us, because we do not wish to have fresh wrongs to avenge, or interests again compromised to defend. We have already withdrawn some of our troops, and we shall recall them all gradually, according to the re-establishment of order and the pacification of the country. We look forward with the sincerest wishes to the day when the last French soldier shall quit Mexico. Those whom our presence disturbs or incommodes may contribute to the approach of that moment. There can be no doubt that excitements from outside keep up agitation. Let those encouragements cease; let them allow that unfortunate country, weary of anarchy, to become tranquil and organize itself under a government calculated to heal the wounds inflicted; order and tranquillity will soon be established, and the term assigned for our occupation will be greatly abridged. But the fact should be well borne in mind that we are not in the habit of hastening our steps on account of haughty injunctions or threatening insinuations.

"You will have the goodness, Monsieur le Marquis, to take in the full meaning of this dispatch, and to communicate those explanations to the Federal government. They have for object, and we desire that they should have for effect, to clear up the situations and remove all doubts as to our intentions. We hope for a reply in the same spirit of frankness and conciliation that has dictated our own language. It is not worthy of two great nations to allow any thing equivocal to subsist between them, and their governments would incur a severe blame in history, and a grave responsibility at the present time, if, in default of preliminary explanation, they were to abandon to the chance of circumstances and unforeseen incidents the maintenance of their good relations and the preservation of peace. Confident in the straightforward common sense of the American people and the enlightened sagacity of its government, we are unwilling to believe that temporary impulses can, against all that is common to us both in old reminiscences, against present interests and future prospects, prevent a truly solid and durable basis for the alliance between the two countries.

"Receive, etc., DROUYN DE LHUYS."

III.

"MR. SEWARD TO MARQUIS DE MONTHOLON.

"DEPARTMENT OF STATE,
"WASHINGTON, *February* 12, 1866.

"SIR:—On the 6th of December I had the honor to submit to you in writing, for the information of the Emperor, a communication upon the subject of affairs in Mexico, as affected by the presence of French armed forces in that country. On the 29th of January thereafter you favored me with a reply to that communication, which reply had been transmitted to you by M. Drouyn de Lhuys, under the date of the 9th of the same month. I have submitted it to the President of the United States. It is now made my duty to revert to the interesting question which has thus been brought under discussion.

"In the first place I take notice of the points which are made by M. Drouyn de Lhuys.

"He declares that the French expedition into Mexico had in it nothing hostile to the institutions of the New World, and still less of any thing hostile to the United States. As proofs of this friendly statement, he refers to the aid in blood and treasure which France contributed in our revolutionary war to the cause of our national independence: to the preliminary proposition that France made to us that we should join her in her expedition to Mexico; and, finally, to the neutrality which France has practiced in the painful civil war through which we have just successfully passed. It gives me pleasure to acknowledge that the assurances thus given on the present occasion that the French expedition, in its original design, had no political objects or motives, harmonize entirely with expressions which abound in the earlier correspondence of the minister of foreign affairs, which arose out of the war between France and Mexico.

"We accept with especial pleasure the reminiscences of our traditional friendship.

"M. Drouyn de Lhuys next assures us that the French government is disposed to hasten, as much as possible the recall of its troops from Mexico. We hail the announcement as being a virtual promise of relief to this government from the apprehensions and anxieties which were the burden of that communication of mine, which M. Drouyn de Lhuys has had under consideration.

"M. Drouyn de Lhuys proceeds to declare that the only aim of France, in pursuing her enterprise in Mexico, has been to follow up the satisfaction to which she had a right after having resorted to coercive measures, when measures of every other form had been exhausted. M. Drouyn Lhuys says that it is known how many and legitimate were the claims of French subjects which caused the resort to arms. He then reminds us how, on a former occasion, the United States had waged war on Mexico. On this point it seems equally necessary and proper to say, that the war thus referred to was not made nor sought by the United States, but was accepted by them under provocations of a very grave character. The transaction is past, and the necessity and justice of the proceedings of the United States are questions which now rest only within the province of history. France, I think, will acknowledge, that neither in the beginning of our Mexican war nor in its prosecution, nor in the terms on which we retired from that successful contest, did the United States assume any position inconsistent with the principles which are now maintained by us in regard to the French expedition in Mexico.

"We are, as we have been, in relations of amity and friendship equally with France and with Mexico, and, therefore, we cannot, consistently with those relations, constitute ourselves a judge of the original merits of the war which is waged between them. We can speak concerning that war only so far as we are affected by its bearing upon ourselves and upon republican and American institutions on this continent.

"M. Drouyn de Lhuys declares that the French army, in entering Mexico, did not carry monarchical traditions in the folds of its flag. In this connexion he refers to the fact that there were, at the time of the expedition a number of influential men in Mexico who despaired of obtaining order out of the conditions of the republican rule then existing there, and who, therefore, cherished the idea of falling back upon monarchy. In this connexion, we are further reminded that one of the later presidents of Mexico offered to use his power for the re-establishment of royalty. We are further informed that at the time of the French invasion, the persons before referred to deemed the moment to have arrived for making an appeal to the people of Mexico in favor of monarchy. M. Drouyn de Lhuys remarks that the French government did not deem it a duty to discourage that supreme effort of a powerful party, which had its origin long anterior to the French expedition.

"M. Drouyn de Lhuys observes that the Emperor faithful to maxims of public right, which he holds in common with the United States, declared on that occasion that the question of change of institutions rested solely on the suffrages of the Mexican people. In support of this statement, M. Drouyn de Lhuys gives us a copy of a letter which the Emperor addressed to the commander-in-chief of the French expedition, on the capture of Puebla, which letter contained the following words: 'Our object, you know, is not to impose on the Mexicans a government against their will, nor to make our success aid the triumph of any party whatsoever. I desire that Mexico may rise to a new life, and that, soon regenerated by a government founded on the national will, on principles of order and of progress, and of respect for the laws of nations, she may acknowledge by her friendly relations that she owes to France her repose and her prosperity.'

"M. Drouyn de Lhuys pursues his argument by saying that the Mexican people have spoken; that the Emperor Maximilian has been called by the voice of the country; that his government has appeared to the Emperor of the French to be of a nature adequate to restore peace to the nation, and, on its part, peace to international relations, and that he has, therefore, given it his support. M. Drouyn de Lhuys thereupon presents the following as a true statement of the present case: France went to Mexico to exercise the right of war, which is exercised by the United States, and not in virtue of any purpose of intervention, concerning which she recognizes the same doctrine with the United States. France went there not to bring about a monarchical proselytism, but to obtain reparations and guarantees which she ought to claim; and, being there, she now sustains the government which is founded on the consent of the people, because she expects from that government the just satisfaction of her wrongs, as well as the securities indispensable to the future. As she does not seek the satisfaction of an exclusive interest, nor the realization of any ambitious schemes, so she now wishes to recall what remains in Mexico of the army corps which France has sent there at the moment when she will be able to do so with safety to French citizens and with due respect for herself.

"I am aware how delicate the discussion is to which M. Drouyn de Lhuys thus invites me. France is entitled, by every consideration of respect and friendship, to interpret for herself the objects of the expedition, and of the whole of her proceedings in Mexico. Her explanation of those motives and objects is, therefore, accepted on our part with the consideration and confidence which we expect for explanations of our own when assigned to France or any other friendly power. Nevertheless, it is my duty to insist that, whatever were the intentions, purposes, and objects of France, the proceedings which were adopted by a class of Mexicans for subverting the republican government there, and for availing themselves of French intervention to establish on its ruins an imperial monarchy, are regarded by the United States as having been taken without the authority, and prosecuted against the will and opinions of the Mexican people. For these reasons it seems to this government that, in supporting institutions thus established in derogation of the inalienable rights of the people of Mexico, the original purposes and objects of the French expedition, though they have not been, as a military demand of satisfaction, abandoned, nor lost out of view by the Emperor of the French, were, nevertheless, left to fall into a condition in which they seem to have become subordinate to a political revolution, which certainly would have not occurred if France had not forcibly intervened, and which, judging from the genius and character of the Mexican people, would not now be maintained by them if that armed intervention should cease. The United States have not seen any satisfactory evidence that the people of Mexico have spoken, and have called into being, or accepted, the so-called empire, which it is insisted has been set up in their capital. The United States, as I have remarked on other occasions, are of opinion that such an acceptance could not have been freely procured or lawfully taken at any time in the presence of the French army of invasion. The withdrawal of the French forces is deemed necessary to allow such a proceeding to be taken by Mexico. Of course the Emperor of France is entitled to determine the aspect in which the Mexican situation ought to be regarded by him. Nevertheless, the view which I have thus presented is the one which this nation has accepted. It therefore recognizes, and must continue to recognize in Mexico, only the ancient republic, and it can in no case consent to involve itself, either directly or indirectly, in relation with or recognition of the institution of the Prince Maximilian in Mexico.

"This position is held, I believe, without one dissenting voice by our countrymen. I do not presume to say that this opinion of the American people is accepted or will be adopted generally by other foreign powers, or by the public opinion of mankind. The Emperor is quite competent to form a judgment upon this important point for himself. I cannot, however, properly exclude the observation that, while this question affects by its bearings, incidentally, every republican State in the American hemisphere, every one of those States has adopted the judgment which, on the behalf of the United States, is herein expressed. Under these circumstances it has happened, either rightfully or wrongfully, that the presence of European armies in Mexico, maintaining a European prince with imperial attributes, without her consent and against her will, is deemed a source of apprehension and danger, not alone to the

United States, but also to all the independent and sovereign republican States founded on the American continent and its adjacent islands. France is acquainted with the relations of the United States toward the other American States to which I have referred, and is aware of the sense that the American people entertain in regard to the obligations and duties due from them to those other States. We are thus brought back to the single question which formed the subject of my communication of the 6th of December last, namely, the desirableness of an adjustment of a question the continuance of which must be necessarily prejudicial to the harmony and friendship which have hitherto always existed between the United States and France.

"This government does not undertake to say how the claims of indemnity and satisfaction, for which the war which France is waging in Mexico was originally instituted, shall now be adjusted, in discontinuing what, in its progress, has become a war of political intervention dangerous to the United States and to republican institutions in the American hemisphere. Recognizing France and the republic of Mexico as belligerents engaged in war, we leave all questions concerning those claims and indemnities to them. The United States rest content with submitting to France the exigencies of an embarrassing situation in Mexico, and expressing the hope that France may find some manner which shall at once be consistent with her interest and honor, and with the principles and interest of the United States, to relieve that situation without injurious delay.

"M. Drouyn de Lhuys repeats on this occasion what he has heretofore written, namely, that it depends much upon the Federal government to facilitate their desire of the withdrawal of the French forces from Mexico. He argues that the position which the United States have assumed has nothing incompatible with the existence of monarchical institutions in Mexico. He draws to his support on this point the fact that the President of the United States, as well as the Secretary of State, in official papers, disclaim all thought of propagandism on the American continent in favor of republican institutions. M. Drouyn de Lhuys draws in, also, the fact that the United States hold friendly relations with the Emperor of Brazil, as they held similar relations with Iturbide, the Mexican Emperor, in 1822. From these positions M. Drouyn de Lhuys makes the deduction that neither any fundamental maxim, nor any precedent in the diplomatic history of this country, creates any necessary antagonism between the United States and the form of government over which the Prince Maximilian presides in the ancient capital of Mexico.

"I do not think it would be profitable, and therefore I am not desirous to engage in the discussions which M. Drouyn de Lhuys has thus raised. It will be sufficient for my purpose, on the present occasion, to assert and to give reassurance of our desire to facilitate the withdrawal of the French troops from Mexico, and, for that purpose, to do whatsoever shall be compatible with the positions we have heretofore taken upon that subject, and with our just regard to the sovereign rights of the republic of Mexico. Further or otherwise than this France could not expect us to go. Having thus reassured France, it seems necessary to state anew the position of this government, as it was set forth in my letter of the 6th of December, as follows: Republican and domestic institutions on this continent are deemed most congenial with and most beneficial to the United States. Where the people of any country, like Brazil now, or Mexico in 1822, have voluntarily established and acquiesced in monarchical institutions of their own choice, free from all foreign control or intervention, the United States do not refuse to maintain relations with such governments, or seek through propagandism, by force or intrigue, to overthrow those institutions. On the contrary, where a nation has established institutions republican and domestic, similar to our own, the United States assert in their behalf that no foreign nation can rightfully intervene by force to subvert republican institutions and establish those of an antagonistical character.

"M. Drouyn de Lhuys seems to think that I have made a double reproach against the Prince Maximilian's alleged government, of the difficulty it encounters and of the assistance it borrows from foreign powers. In that respect M. Drouyn de Lhuys contends that the obstacles and the resistance which Maximilian has been obliged to wrestle with have in themselves nothing especial against the form of the institutions which he is supposed by M. Drouyn de Lhuys to have established.

M. Drouyn de Lhuys maintains that Maximilian's government is undergoing the lot quite common to new powers, while, above all, it has the misfortune to have to bear the consequences of discords which have been produced under a previous government. M. Drouyn de Lhuys represents this misfortune and this lot to be in effect the misfortune and lot of governments which have not found armed competitors, and which have enjoyed in peace an uncontrolled authority. M. Drouyn de Lhuys alleges that revolts and intestine wars are the normal condition of Mexico, and he further insists that the opposition made by some military chiefs to the establishment of an empire under Maximilian is only the natural sequence of the same want of discipline, and the same prevalence of anarchy, of which his predecessors in power in Mexico have been victims. It is not the purpose, nor would it be consistent with the character of the United States, to deny that Mexico has been for a long time the theatre of faction and intestine war. The United States confess this fact with regret, all the more sincere, because the experience of Mexico has been not only painful for her own people, but has been also of unfortunate evil influence on other nations.

"On the other hand, it is neither a right of the United States, nor consistent with their friendly disposition toward Mexico, to reproach the people of that country with her past calamities, much less to invoke or approve of the infliction of punishment upon them by strangers for their political errors. The Mexican population have, and their situation has, some peculiarities which are doubtless well understood by France. Early in the present century they were forced, by convictions which mankind cannot but respect, to cast off a foreign monarchical rule which they deemed incompatible with their welfare and aggrandizement. They were forced, at the same time, by convictions which the world must respect, to attempt the establishment of republican institutions, without the full experience and practical education and habits which would render those institutions all at once firm and satisfactory. Mexico was a theatre of conflict between European commercial, ecclesiastical, and political institutions and dogmas, and novel American institutions and ideas. She had African slavery, colonial restrictions, and ecclesiastical monopolies. In the chief one of these particulars she had a misfortune which was shared by the United States, while the latter were happily exempted from the other misfortunes. We cannot forget that Mexico, sooner and more readily than the United States, abolished slavery. We cannot deny that all the anarchy in Mexico, of which M. Drouyn de Lhuys complains, was necessarily, and even wisely, endured in the attempts to lay sure foundations of broad republican liberty.

"I do not know whether France can rightfully be expected to concur in this view, which alleviates, in our mind, the errors, misfortunes, and calamities of Mexico. However this may be, we fall back upon the principle that no foreign State can rightly intervene in such trials as those of Mexico, and, on the ground of a desire to correct those errors, deprive the people there of their natural right of domestic and republican freedom. All the injuries and wrongs which Mexico can have committed against any other State have found a severe punishment in consequences which legitimately followed their commission. Nations are not authorized to correct each other's errors, except so far as is necessary to prevent or redress injuries affecting themselves. If one State has a right to intervene in any other State, to establish discipline, constituting itself a judge of the occasion, then every State has the same right to intervene in the affairs of every other nation, being itself alone the arbiter, both in regard to the time and the occasion. The principle of intervention, thus practically carried out, would seem to render all sovereignty and independence, and even all international peace and amity, uncertain and fallacious.

"M. Drouyn de Lhuys proceeds to remark, that as for the support which Maximilian receives from the French army, as well also for the support which has been lent him by Belgian and Austrian volunteers, those supports cause no hindrance to the freedom of his resolutions in the affairs of his government. M. Drouyn de Lhuys asks what State is there that does not need allies, either to form or to defend? As to the great powers, such as France and England, do they not constantly maintain foreign troops in their armies? When the United States fought for their independence, did the aid given by France cause that movement to cease to be truly national? Shall it be said that the contest between the United States and the recent insurgents was not in a like manner a national war, because thousands of Irishmen and Germans were found fighting under the flag of the Union? Arguing from anticipated answers to these questions, M. Drouyn de Lhuys reaches a conclusion that the character of Maximilian's government cannot be contested, nor can its efforts to consolidate itself be contested, on the ground of the employment of foreign troops.

"M. Drouyn de Lhuys, in this argument, seems to us to have overlooked two important facts, namely: first, that the United States, in this correspondence, have assigned definite limits to the right of alliance incompatible with our assent to his argument; and secondly, the fact that the United States have not at any time accepted the supposed government of the Prince Maximilian as a constitutional or legitmate form of government in Mexico, capable or entitled to form alliances.

"M. Drouyn de Lhuys then arranges, in a graphic manner, the advantages that have arisen, or are to arise, to the United States, from the successful establishment of the supposed empire in Mexico. Instead of a country unceasingly in trouble, and which has given us so many subjects of complaint, and against which we ourselves have been obliged to make war, he shows us in Mexico a pacific country, under a beneficent imperial sway, offering henceforth measures of security and vast openings to our commerce, a country far from injuring our rights and hurting our influences. And he assures us that, above all other nations, the United States are most likely to profit by the work which is being accomplished by Prince Maximilian in Mexico. These suggestions are as natural on the part of France as they are friendly to the United States. The United States are not insensible to the desirableness of political and commercial reform in the adjoining country; but their settled principles, habits, and convictions forbid them to look for such changes in this hemisphere to foreign, royal, or imperial institutions, founded upon a forcible subversion of republican institutions. The United States, in their customary sobriety, regard no beneficial results which could come from such a change in Mexico as sufficient to overbalance the injury which they must directly suffer by the overthrow of the republican government in Mexico.

"M. Drouyn de Lhuys, at the end of his very elaborate and able review, recapitulates his exposition in the following words: 'The United States acknowledge the right we had to make war in Mexico. On the other part, we admit, as they do, the principle of non-intervention. This double postulate includes, as it seems to me, the elements of an agreement. The right to make war, which belongs, as Mr. Seward declares, to every sovereign nation, implies the right to secure the results of war. We have not gone across the ocean merely for the purpose of showing our power, and of inflicting chastisement on the Mexican government. After a train of fruitless remonstrances, it was our duty to demand guarantees against the recurrence of violence from which our country had suffered so cruelly, and those guarantees we could not look for from a government whose bad faith we had proved on so many occasions. We find them now engaged in the establishment of a regular government which shows itself disposed to honestly keep its engagements. In this relation we hope that the legitimate object of our expedition will soon be reached, and we are striving to make with the Emperor Maximilian arranguments which, by satisfying our interests and our honor, will permit us to consider at an end the service of the army upon Mexican soil. The Emperor has given an order to write in this same sense to our minister at Mexico. We fall back at that moment on the principle of non-intervention, and from that moment accept it as the rule of our conduct. Our interest, no less than our honor, commands us to claim from all the uniform application of it. Trusting the spirit of equity which animates the cabinet of Washington, we expect from it the assurance that the American people will themselves conform to the law which they invoke, by observing, in regard to Mexico, a strict neutrality. When you [meaning the Marquis de Montholon] shall have informed me of the resolution of the Federal government, I shall be able to indicate to you the nature of the results of our negotiation with the Emperor Maximilian for the return of our troops.'

"I have already, and not without much reluctance, made the comments upon the arguments of M. Drouyn de Lhuys which seem to be necessary to guard against the inference of concurrence in questionable positions which might be drawn from our entire silence. I think that I can, therefore, afford to leave his recapitulation of those arguments without such an especial review as would necessarily be prolix, and perhaps hypercritical. The United States have not claimed, and they do not claim, to know what arrangements the Emperor may make for the adjustment of claims for indemnity and redress in Mexico. It would be, on our part, an act of intervention to take cognizance of them. We adhere to our position that the war in question has become a political war between France and the republic of Mexico, injurious and dangerous to the United States and to the republican cause, and we ask only that in that aspect and character it may be brought to an end. It would be illiberal on the part of the United States to suppose that, in desiring or pursuing preliminary arrangements, the Emperor contemplates the establishment in Mexico, before withdrawing his forces, of the very institutions which constitute the material ground of the exceptions taken against his intervention by the United States. It would be still more illiberal to suppose for a moment that he expects the United States to bind themselves indirectly to acquiesce in or support the obnoxious institutions.

"On the contrary, we understand him as announcing to us his immediate purpose to bring to an end the service of his armies in Mexico, to withdraw them, and in good faith to fall back, without stipulation or condition on our part, upon the principle of non-intervention upon which he is henceforth agreed with the United States. We cannot understand his appeal to us for an assurance that we ourselves will abide by our own principles of non-intervention in any other sense than as the expression, in a friendly way, of his expectation that when the people of Mexico shall have been left absolutely free from the operation, effects, and consequences of his own political and military intervention, we will ourselves respect their self-established sovereignty and independence. In this view of the subject only can we consider his appeal pertinent to the case. Regarding it in only this aspect, we must meet the Emperor frankly. He knows the form and character of this government. The nation can be bound only by treaties which have the concurrence of the President and two thirds of the Senate. A formal treaty would be objectionable as unnecessary, except as a disavowal of bad faith on our part, to disarm suspicion in regard to a matter concerning which we have given no cause for questioning our loyalty, or else such a treaty would be refused upon the ground that the application for it by the Emperor of France was unhappily a suggestion of some sinister or unfriendly reservation or purpose on his part in withdrawing from Mexico. Diplomatic assurances given by the President in behalf of the nation can at best be but the expressions of confident expectation on his part that the personal administration, ever changing in conformity and adaptation to the national will, does not misunderstand the settled principles and policy of the American people. Explanations cannot properly be made by the President in any case wherein it would be deemed, for any reason, objectionable on grounds of public policy by the treaty-making power of the government to introduce or entertain negotiations.

"With these explanations I proceed to say that, in the opinion of the President, France need not for a moment delay her promised withdrawal of military forces from Mexico, and her putting the principle of non-intervention into full and complete practice in regard to Mexico, through any apprehension that the United States will prove unfaithful to the principles and policy in that respect which, on their behalf, it has been my duty to maintain in this now very lengthened correspondence. The practice of this government, from its beginning, is a guarantee to all nations of the respect of the American people for the free sovereignty of the people in every other State. We received the instruction from Washington. We applied it sternly in our early intercourse even with France. The same principle and practice have been uniformly inculcated by all our statesmen, interpreted by all our jurists, maintained by all our Congresses, and acquiesced in without practical dissent on all occasions by the American people. It is in reality the chief element of foreign intercourse in our history. Looking simply toward the point to which our attention has been steadily confined, the relief of the Mexican embarrassments without disturbing our relations with France, we shall be gratified when the Emperor shall give to us, either through the channel of your esteemed correspondence or otherwise, definitive information of the time when French military operations may be expected to cease in Mexico.

"Here I might perhaps properly conclude this note. Some obscurity, however, might be supposed to rest upon the character of the principle of non-intervention, which we are authorized to suppose is now agreed upon between the United States and France as a rule for their future government in regard to Mexico. I shall, therefore, reproduce on this occasion, by way of illustration, some of the forms in which that principle has been maintained by us in our previous intercourse with France. In 1861, when alluding to the possibility that the Emperor might be invoked by rebel emissaries from the United States to intervene in our civil war, I observed: 'The Emperor of France has given abundant proofs that he considers the people in every country the rightful source of authority, and that its only legitimate objects are their safety, freedom, and welfare.'

"I wrote also, on the same occasion, these words to Mr. Dayton: 'I have thus, under the President's direction, placed before you a simple, unexaggerated, and dispassionate statement of the origin, nature, and purposes of the contest in which the United States are now involved. I have done so only for the purpose of deducing from it the arguments you will find it necessary to employ in opposing the application of the so-called Confederate States to the government of his majesty the Emperor for a recognition of their independence and sovereignty. The President neither expects nor desires any intervention, or even any favor, from the government of France, or any other, in this emergency. Whatever else he may consent to do, he will never invoke nor even admit foreign interference or influence in this or any other controversy in which the government of the United States may be engaged with any portion of the American people.'

* * * * * *

"'Foreign intervention would oblige us to treat those who should yield it as allies of the insurrectionary party, and to carry on the war against them as enemies.

"'However other European powers may mistake, his majesty is the last one of those sovereigns to misapprehend the nature of this controversy. He knows that the revolution of 1776, in this country, was a successful contest of the great American idea of free, popular government against resisting prejudices and errors. He knows that the conflict awakened the sympathies of mankind, and that ultimately the triumph of that idea has been hailed by all European nations He knows at what cost European nations for a time resisted the progress of that idea, and, perhaps, is not unwilling to confess how much France, especially, has profited by it. He will not fail to recognize the presence of that one great idea in the present conflict, nor will he mistake the side on which it will be found. It is, in short, the very principle of universal suffrage, with its claim of obedience to its decrees, on which the government of France is built that is put in issue by the insurrection here, and is in this emergency to be vindicated and more effectually than ever established by the government of the United States.'

"In writing upon the same subject to Mr. Dayton,

on the 30th of May, 1861, I said: 'Nothing is wanting to that success except that foreign nations shall leave us, as is our right, to manage our own affairs in our own way. They, as well as we, can only suffer by their intervention. No one, we are sure, can judge better than the Emperor of France how dangerous and deplorable would be the emergency that should intrude Europeans into the political contests of the American people.'

"In declining the offer of French mediation, on the 8th of June, 1861, I wrote to Mr. Dayton: 'The present paramount duty of the government is to save the integrity of the American Union. Absolute, self-sustaining independence is the first and most indispensable element of national existence. This is a republican nation; all its domestic affairs must be conducted and even adjusted in constitutional forms, and upon constitutional, republican principles. This is an American nation, and its internal affairs must not only be conducted with reference to its peculiar continental position, but by and through American agencies alone.'

"On the 1st of August, 1862, Mr. Adams was instructed by this government in the following words: 'Did the European States which found and occupied this continent almost without effort then understand its real destiny and purposes? Have they ever yet fully understood and accepted them? Has anything but disappointment, upon disappointment and disaster upon disaster, resulted from their misapprehensions? After near four hundred years of such disappointments and disasters, is the way of Providence in regard to America still so mysterious that it cannot be understood and confessed? Columbus, it was said, had given a new world to the kingdoms of Castile and Leon. What has become of the sovereignty of Spain in America? Richelieu occupied and fortified a large portion of the continent, extending from the Gulf of Mexico to the straits of Belle Isle. Does France yet retain that important appendage to the crown of her sovereign? Great Britan acquired a dominion here surpassing by a hundred-fold in length and breadth the native realm. Has not a large portion of it been already formally resigned? To whom have those vast dominions, with those founded by the Portuguese, the Dutch, and the Swedes, been resigned but to American nations, the growth of European colonists and exiles, who have come hither, bringing with them the arts, the civilization, and the virtues of Europe? Has not the change been beneficial to society on this continent? Has it not been more beneficial even to Europe itself than continued European domination, if it had been possible, could have been? The American nations which have grown up here are free and self-governing. They have made themselves so from inherent vigor and in obedience to absolute necessity. Is it possible for European States to plunge them again into a colonial state and hold them there? Would it be desirable for them and for Europe, if it were possible? The balance of power among the nations of Europe is maintained not without numerous strong armies and frequent conflicts, while the sphere of political ambition there is bounded by the ocean which surrounds that continent. Would it be possible to maintain it at all, if this vast continent, with all its populations, their resources, and their forces, should once again be brought within that sphere?

"'On the contrary of all these suppositions, is it not manifest that these American nations were called into existence to be the home of freemen; that the States of Europe have been intrusted by Providence with their tutelage, but that tutelage and all its responsibilities and powers are necessarily withdrawn to the relief and benefit of the parties and of mankind, when these parties become able to choose their own system of government, and to make and administer their own laws? If they err in this choice, or in the conduct of their affairs, it will be found wise to leave them, like all other States, the privilege and responsibility of detecting and correcting the error by which they are, of course, the principal sufferers.'

"On the 8th of May, 1862, Mr. Dayton was instructed to express to M. Thouvenel 'the desire of the United States that peaceful relations may soon be restored between France and Mexico upon a basis just to both parties, and favorable to the independence and sovereignty of the people of Mexico, which is equally the interest of France and all other enlightened nations.'

"On the 21st of June, 1862, Mr. Dayton was authorized to speak on behalf of the United States concerning the condition of Mexico in these words: 'France has a right to make war against Mexico, and to determine for herself the cause. We have a right to insist that France shall not improve the war she makes to raise up in Mexico an anti-republican or anti-American government, or to maintain such a government there.'

"Accept, sir, a renewed assurance of my high consideration.

"WILLIAM H. SEWARD.

"The MARQUIS DE MONTHOLON, etc., etc."

IV.

MR. DROUYN DE LHUYS TO THE MARQUIS DE MONTHOLON.

"[Translation.]

"PARIS, *April* 5, 1866.

"SIR:—I have read, with all the attention which it deserves, the answer of the Secretary of State to my dispatch of the 9th of January last. The scrupulous care with which Mr. Seward has pleased to analyze that dispatch, and the extended considerations upon which he has entered to define, in regard to the expose which I have made of the conduct of France in the affairs of Mexico, the doctrines which are the basis of the international policy of the United States, bear witness in our eyes of the interest which the cabinet of Washington attaches to putting aside all misapprehension.

"We find therein the evidence of its desire to cause the sentiments of amity which the traditions of a long alliance have cemented between our two countries to prevail over the accidental divergencies, often inevitable, in the movement of affairs and the relations of governments. It is in this disposition that we have appreciated the communication which the Secretary of State has addressed to you, the 12th of February last. I will not follow Mr. Seward in the developments he has given to the exposition of the principles which direct the policy of the American Union. It does not appear to me opportune or profitable to prolong, on points of doctrine or of history, a discussion, where we may differ in opinion from the government of the United States, without danger to the interests of the two countries. I think it better to serve those interests by abstaining from discussing assertions—in my opinion very contestable—in order to take action on assurances which may contribute to faciliate our understanding.

"We never hesitate to offer to our friends the explanations they ask from us, and we hasten to give to the cabinet of Washington all those which may enlighten it on the purpose we are pursuing in Mexico, and on the loyalty of our intentions. We have said to it, at the same time, that the certainty we should acquire of its resolution to observe in regard to that country, after our departure, a policy of non-intervention, would hasten the moment when it would be possible for us, without compromising the interests which led us there, to withdraw our troops, and put an end to an occupation, the duration of which we are sincerely desirous to abridge. In his dispatch of the 12th of February last Mr. Seward calls to mind, on his part, that the government of the United States has conformed during the whole course of its history to the rule of conduct which it received from Washington, by practicing invariably the principle of non-intervention, and adds that nothing justifies the apprehension that it should show itself unfaithful in what may concern Mexico. We receive this assurance with entire confidence, and we find therein a sufficient guarantee not any longer to delay the adoption of measures intended to prepare for the return of our army. The Emperor has decided that the French troops shall evacuate Mexico in three detachments: the first being intended to depart in the month of November, 1866; the second in March, 1867; and the third in the month of November of the same year.

"You will please to communicate this decision officially to the Secretary of State.

"Receive, Marquis, the assurance of my high consideration.

"DROUYN DE LHUYS.

"The Marquis de Montholon,
"*Minister of the Emperor, at Washington.*"

V.

"MR. SEWARD TO MR. BIGELOW.

"DEPARTMENT OF STATE.
"WASHINGTON, *Nov.* 23, 1866.

"SIR:—Your dispatch of the 8th of November (No. 384), in regard to Mexico, is received. Your proceedings in your interview with M. Moustier, and also your proceedings in your interview with the Emperor, are entirely approved. Say to M. Moustier that this government is surprised and affected with deep concern by the announcement now made for the first time that the promised recall of one detachment of the French troops from Mexico in November current has been postponed by the Emperor. The embarrassment thus produced is immeasurably increased by the circumstance that this proceeding of the Emperor has been taken without conference with and even without notice to the United States. This government has not in any way afforded reinforcements to the Mexicans, as the Emperor seems to assume, and it has known nothing at all of his countermanding instructions to Marshal Bazaine, of which the Emperor speaks. We consult only official communication to ascertain the purpose and resolutions of France, as we make our own purposes and resolutions known only in the same manner when she is concerned. I am not prepared to say, and it is now unnecessary to discuss, whether the President could or could not have agreed to the Emperor's proposed delay, if he had been seasonably consulted—if the proposition had been then put, as the proceeding is now, upon the ground of military considerations alone, and if it had been marked with the customary manifestations of regard to the interests and feelings of the United States. But the Emperor's decision to modify the existing arrangement without any understanding with the United States, so as to leave the whole French army in Mexico for the present, instead of withdrawing one detachment in November current, as promised, is now found in every way inconvenient and exceptionable. We cannot acquiesce, first, because the term "next spring," as appointed for the entire evacuation, is indefinite and vague; second, because we have no authority for stating to Congress and to the American people, that we have now a better guarantee for the withdrawal of the whole expeditionary force in the spring than we have heretofore had for the withdrawal of a part in November; third, in full reliance upon at least a literal performance of the Emperor's existing agreement we have taken measures, while facilitating the anticipated French evacuation to co-operate with the republican government of Mexico for promoting the pacification of that country, and for the early and complete restoration of the proper constitutional authority of that government. As a part of those measures, Mr. Campbell, our newly appointed Minister, attended by Lieutenant-general Sherman, has been sent to Mexico in order to confer with President Juarez on subjects which are deeply interesting to the United States, and of vital importance to Mexico. Our policy and measures thus adopted in full reliance upon the anticipated beginning of the evacuation of Mexico were promptly made known to the French legation here, and doubtless you have already executed your instructions by making them known to the Emperor's government in Paris. The Emperor will perceive that we cannot now recall Mr. Campbell: nor can we modify the instructions under which he is expected to treat, and under which he may even now be treating with the republican government of Mexico. That government will of course most earnestly desire and confidently expect an early and entire discontinuation of foreign hostile occupation. You will therefore state to the Emperor's government, that the President sincerely hopes and expects that the evacuation of Mexico will be carried into effect with such conformity to the existing agreement as the inopportune complication which calls for this dispatch shall allow. Mr. Campbell will be advised of that complication. Instructions will be issued to the United States military forces of observation to await in every case special directions from the President. This will be done with a confident expectation that the telegraph or the mail may seasonably bring us a satisfactory resolution from the Emperor in reply to this note. You will assure the French government that the United States, while they seek the relief of Mexico, desire nothing more earnestly than to preserve peace and friendship with France; nor does the President allow himself to doubt that what has been determined in France, most inauspiciously, as we think, has been decided upon inadvertently, without full reflection upon the embarrassment it must produce here, and without any design to retain the French expeditionary forces in Mexico beyond the full period of eighteen months originally stipulated for the complete evacuation.

"I am, sir, your obedient servant,

"WILLIAM H. SEWARD.

"To John Bigelow, Esq., &c., Paris."

www.ingramcontent.com/pod-product-compliance
Lightning Source LLC
LaVergne TN
LVHW010250110826
845151LV00004B/1436

* 9 7 8 1 4 2 5 5 2 3 0 9 1 *